An Education

An Education

Lynn Barber

ATLAS & CO.

Atlas & Co. *Publishers*
15 West 26th Street, 2nd floor
New York, NY 10010
www.atlasandco.com

Distributed to the trade by W. W. Norton & Company

Printed in the United States

Library of Congress Cataloging-in-Publication Data
is available upon request

First published in the United Kingdom by the Penguin Group

The moral right of the author has been asserted

'Tarantella' by Hilaire Belloc from *Sonnets and Verses*
(© The Estate of Hilaire Belloc 1923) is reproduced by permission of PFD
(www.pfd.co.uk) on behalf of The Estate of Hilaire Belloc.

An extract from 'Sea Fever' by John Masefield is reproduced
by permission of The Society of Authors and the literary
representative of the Estate of John Masefield.

Interior design and typesetting by
Palimpsest Book Production Limited, Grangemouth, Stirlingshire

Atlas & Company books may be purchased for educational,
business, or sales promotional use. For information, please
write to info@atlasandco.com.

ISBN: 978-1-934633-85-4

14   13   12   11   10   2   3   4   5   6

For Rosie and Theo

Contents

Childhood

I know memoirs are supposed to begin with ancestors but alas, I don't have any, because I come from the lower, unremembered, orders on both sides. There is no Barber ancestral seat, nor even, so far as I know, any Barber ancestral village. The only remotely distinguished ancestor I ever heard of was a great-great-uncle on my mother's side who was stationmaster at Swaffham in Norfolk. Of course being a stationmaster was quite a big deal in Victorian times, and I remember once seeing a sepia photo of him in his stationmaster's uniform which was indeed very grand, but I don't think I need tax you (or myself) with any Swaffham stationmaster research.

The other day, driving down the M3, I saw a turn-off to Bagshot and thought, 'My birthplace! Maybe I should go and see it?' But by the time I'd debated the pros and cons, I was miles past the turn-off so Bagshot, like the stationmaster, remains unknown. I was only born there because my mother was staying with her parents in Sunningdale, Berkshire, and Bagshot was the nearest maternity home. No doubt it is a charming and salubrious place but all I know about it is that I was born there, on 22 May 1944, and survived.

My mother was staying with her parents because my father was still away 'fighting the war' or actually mending tank wirelesses in Catterick. He had such bad eyesight he was never sent on active service, but spent an uneventful war in England. He met my mother when they were both stationed in Birmingham, she driving ambulances, he guarding a mental hospital. He tells me she was the most glamorous woman he'd ever seen in his life – and that was *before* her teeth fell out. All through her girlhood and twenties, she had terrible goofy sticking-out teeth. But then – as apparently often happened because of calcium deficiency during the war – all her teeth fell out. It was the best thing that could have happened. With her smart new set of non-goofy National Health gnashers, she emerged as a real beauty, often compared to the film star Rosalind Russell. She had thick black wavy hair, hazel eyes, peachy skin, a huge bust and long legs. People must have wondered why such a stunner should marry a bespectacled geek like my father, but the explanation lay in her premarital teeth.

My memories begin after the war when we were living in a rented flat over a shopping parade in Ashford, Middlesex. I can remember seeing a caterpillar on the curtains, and a rat nosing round the dustbins in the yard. But the main thing I remember is that until I was about three there was a big pram in the corner of the sitting room and then one day it wasn't there. I asked my mother where it had gone and she said she'd given it away, but there was an awkwardness in the way she said it that made it memorable. I suppose it was the first intimation that I was to be an only child.

Being an only child is clearly the defining feature of my

character. It meant that I was very lonely for much of my childhood, and relied entirely on books and my imaginary friend Kay for companionship. I didn't have any friends till I was ten or eleven, which was tolerable in term time but painful in the holidays. Worst of all was the annual seaside holiday – a week at a guest house in Lowestoft with my parents – when I would sit on the beach with my nose in a book, envying the other children who played around me. Envying them but also despising them. How could they be so *childish*? I sniffed. Why were they laughing just because they were chasing a ball? But apparently this was what was meant by having fun. I longed for it, but also recognised that I was not cut out for it. Even if the children on the beach had asked me to play (they never did) I wouldn't have known what to do.

I was not only an only child but also, I think, an exceptionally isolated one, because my parents didn't seem to have any friends. My father had his bridge club (he was a county champion), my mother her amateur dramatic society, but if they had friends there, they never brought them home. Nor did we have any relatives in London. My mother was an only child so her only family was her parents. My father did have siblings, two of whom had children, but we rarely saw them because they lived in Lancashire. I longed to be part of a big extended family, a 'tribe', with lots of cousins – I thought cousins would be ideal, much better than brothers or sisters who might encroach on my power. Most of all, I yearned to know, not just other children, but other *families*, to see how they interacted. But I never did, in fact not until I was an adult.

3

My parents were effectively first-generation immigrants to the middle class, having arrived by way of grammar school. My father's family was grindingly poor – his father, a millhand, died of 'inanition' when Dad was four and his mother raised four children on a tiny widow's pension. They lived in Bolton, Lancashire, in the shadow of the textile mills, and Dad remembers the great family treat was going round to his uncle's on Sunday afternoons to eat bowls of mashed potato with gravy left over from the Sunday lunch. Occasionally there was even a bit of meat. He remembers winning a prize at school and going on stage to accept it wearing new boots his mother had managed to obtain for the occasion – but they were bright orange and everybody laughed.

My father won a place at Manchester university to read maths but couldn't afford to take it up – instead he joined the civil service and did a law degree at night school when he came back from the war. I remember when I was very young, Mum saying, 'Shush, Dad's doing his Torts.' I never knew what they were but I knew they were frightening – as finals approached, the back of his neck was covered with flaming boils. He got his law degree and gradually rose through the ranks of the Estate Duty office but, although he had a middle-class salary, he somehow remained working class. He was formidably intelligent but socially untamed. He still said 'Side the pots' in his broad Lancashire accent, whereupon I would say to Mum 'Shall I clear the table?' and she would sigh and say 'You know your father told you to.' We also sighed over his habit of leaving the house with bits of paper stuck to his face when he cut himself shaving. My mother was far more civilised but, as I told my father, she had only a beta or maybe even beta-minus brain.

My mother came from slightly more genteel stock than my father – rural rather than urban, in service rather than in manufacturing, and with the towering figure of the Swaffham stationmaster in the background. Her father (an extremely handsome man) had an invalid pension from being gassed in the First World War, and took occasional jobs as a postman and gardener; her mother was a qualified swimming instructor. They lived in a two-up, two-down cottage in Sunningdale, which was then a country village, and went to Wentworth golf club at weekends to make a few pennies finding lost golf balls. My mother, despite her beta brain, won a scholarship to grammar school and then to the London Academy of Music and Dramatic Art. She hoped to become an actress but settled for a diploma that qualified her to teach elocution, of which more later.

My parents had been raised as Methodists but by the time they had me their religion was education, education, education. I was reared from the cradle to pass every possible exam, gain every possible scholarship, and go to university – Cambridge if I was mathematically inclined like my father, or Oxford if I proved to be 'artistic' like my mother. My father often quoted Charles Kingsley's line 'Be good, sweet maid, and let who can be clever' but he said it sarcastically – he wanted me to be clever, and let who can be good.

My mother taught me to read long before I started

5

school so I was amazed on my first day at Ashford Congregationalist Primary to find myself stuck in a class with ninnies who didn't even know the alphabet. Naturally this attitude made me unpopular with my classmates and I was soon unpopular with the teachers as well because I refused to eat the school food. The school had a rule – as did most schools in those days – that you could not leave the table till you had eaten all your lunch, so some poor teacher would have to waste her break sitting with me, telling me to eat up. I never would. In the end my mother went to see the headmistress and arrived at a satisfactory compromise: I could leave most of my lunch provided I ate *something* and most days I could. But there was one day a week when we had gristle stew which I couldn't eat at all. So on that day I went down the road to the cinema where, in the hushed grandeur of the Odeon restaurant, I ordered soup with roast potatoes and was fussed over by the waitresses. It was my first valuable lesson in the rewards of intransigence.

That is about all I remember from Ashford; my real memories begin when we moved to Twickenham when I was eight. My parents kept saying they had bought this big old house – they were so excited they talked about it endlessly. My idea of big old houses was entirely derived from books like *The Secret Garden* so I pictured a rambling pile with attics and battlements and secret staircases. I worried that I might get lost in the cellars, or that my room in the west wing would be haunted by a headless nun. When I finally saw 52 Clifden Road, Twickenham, I laughed incredulously, 'You said it was *big*!' I can now understand that it *was* big by my parents' standards, a solid Edwardian three-up, three-down terraced house with a porch and a conservatory and longish garden at the back. (Apparently houses in Clifden Road go for almost a million now.) But I persisted in believing my parents had lied to me, and grumbled for years, 'You said it was *big*!'

The house was opposite a girls' school, Twickenham County Grammar, but it only took girls from age eleven, so I had to go to junior school on the other side of town. It was a mixed school, full of rough boys who lurked round the playground lavatories, and jumped up and looked over the door if you went in. Consequently I was terrified of ever going to the loo and developed complicated regimes of what I could eat at what times. For a year – *pace* Aunt Ruth – I ate almost nothing but scrambled eggs on toast. Another year it was Marmite soldiers. Luckily the term 'eating disorders' was unknown then, or my parents might have worried about me – though on second thoughts, they wouldn't have worried about me as long as my school marks were OK, which of course they were. I was paired with the one other bright girl, Margaret M, and we took it in turns to win the class gold star every week – nobody else ever got a look-in. Consequently all the other pupils hated us, and we hated them, but we hated each other more.

The only good thing I remember from those early Twickenham years was the night sweet rationing ended. My parents had taken me to the cinema – we went at least once, often twice, a week and I saw some wonderfully 'unsuitable' films such as *The Barefoot Contessa* ('What does it mean he was wounded in the war, Mum? What sort of wound? Why does it mean he can't marry her?') – but this night I think was a boring one until the lights went up and the manager came onstage and said, 'Ladies and gentlemen, we have heard on the wireless that sweet rationing has ended. We have a full selection of sweets and chocolates in the lobby.' Everyone stampeded for the doors. My father of course didn't. He 'didn't see the point' of sweets, but my mother did and we went and bought packets of toffee and chocolate raisins and ate them till I was sick. Since then, I've never cared much for sweets, but it was an historic occasion.

When I was ten, my parents took the huge financial gamble of sending me to the junior school of Lady Eleanor Holles, an independent fee-paying school some miles away in Hampton. The idea was that if they paid for me to go to the junior school for a year, I would then win a scholarship to the main school – which is what indeed happened. At Lady Eleanor Holles, for the first time, I was mixing with girls from quite wealthy backgrounds – some of them even had their own ponies. I would listen, ears flapping, to their boastful conversations about Daddy's new Jaguar or Mummy's new refrigerator. The snobbery at LEH was all the more fierce because it was conducted within such a tiny social range: the Oxshott girls despised the Ewell girls who despised the Kingston girls; the Jaguar owners despised the Wolseley owners and we all duly gasped when the parents of a rather quiet girl who nobody took any notice of turned up for prize-giving in a Rolls Royce.

I could see that there was no way I could win in the snobbery stakes – we didn't have a car, let alone a paddock – so I didn't bother lying but just told everyone I was a pauper and the cleverest girl in the school, which I probably was. (Apparently Lady Eleanor Holles is a highly academic school nowadays but it certainly wasn't then.) And actually it paid off. The pony-owners found it quite amusing to know me – I was a novelty in their world. And they were very generous: they would always lend me clothes for parties and hand over any book tokens they were given for Christmas on the grounds that they had no conceivable use for them and I did. Consequently I have always found it difficult to hate the rich, as good leftie journalists are meant to do, because they've always been so nice to me. The LEH girls liked having a pauper in their midst, and I liked having friends for the first time in my life. It was a great day for me when we moved up to the main school and *three* girls competed to sit next to me in class. Probably they just hoped to crib my schoolwork, but I basked in my first taste of popularity.

The only thing wrong with LEH from my point of view was that it was surrounded by miles of playing fields and you had to play games. Worst of all you had to play lax – lacrosse – which relied on the daft notion that it was possible to run while holding a ball in a sort of primitive snowshoe above your head while other girls hit you with their snowshoes and tried to trip you up. Obviously it was dangerous folly even to attempt it. And then we had to take communal showers where the dykey games mistress stared longingly at our nascent boobs and bushes. Eventually I got my parents to write a note saying I had weak ankles and should not play games – which would have been fine except that I then had to go to remedial podiatry sessions and learn to pick up pencils with my toes. Then the podiatrist said I should take up ice skating to strengthen my weak ankles and actually got me a free pass to Saturday sessions at Richmond Ice Rink. God – I'd thought lacrosse was scary, ice skating was *terrifying*. In theory there was a quiet place in the middle of the rink where you could practise your figures but you had to get to it through this stampeding pack of speed skaters. I once saw someone's finger sliced off when he fell over in the pack and a ring of blood went right round the rink before the stewards could get the speed skaters to stop.

The other great curse of these years was my mother's elocution lessons. When we lived at Ashford, she had a part-time job at a department store in Windsor teaching shopgirls to speak posh, but when we moved to Twickenham she set up the front room as her 'studio' with her LAMDA certificate on the wall and gave elocution lessons at home. She would have liked to have had a board saying Elocution Lessons on the front gate, but my father and I both vetoed it – my father on the grounds that it might make us liable for business rates; me on the grounds that I would slash my wrists from embarrassment.

In those days – the Fifties – there were elocution teachers in every town; in Twickenham alone, there were at least three, and another half-dozen across the river in Richmond. They claimed to teach drama, 'projection', and the art of public speaking, but what they really taught was how to talk posh, or a particular version thereof. When my mother said of someone 'She has a bit of an accent' she meant, not a regional accent, nor even a cockney accent, but the most fearful accent of all, which was Common. Common meant saying *sumpfink* for something, or dropping your aitches or pronouncing the letter h as *haitch*. 'I had to go to Homerton High Street, your honour, to acquire a hat' was a good test of Common. The aim of elocution lessons was to eradicate Common and teach shopgirls to talk like ladies, though what they invariably ended up talking like was shopgirls with pretensions. At Windsor, my mother actually taught shopgirls to say, 'Would Modom care to try the larger size?'

A trained speaker, my mother always told me, could recite the London telephone directory and make it interesting. (The corollary of this, I noticed in adulthood, is that many actors say their lines as if reciting the London telephone directory, as if the words have no intrinsic meaning at all.) The aim of elocution was to display a grasp of diction, enunciation, inflection, projection, chiarascuro, cadence, timbre, lightness, colour, vibrato, crescendo, diminuendo, while reciting, say,

> All along the backwater,
> Through the rushes tall,
> Ducks are a-dabbling
> Up tails all!
> Ducks' tails, drakes' tails,
> Yellow feet a-quiver,
> Yellow bills all out of sight,

Busy in the river!
('Ducks' Ditty', Kenneth Grahame)

There was much talk of labials and plosives and breathing from the diaphragm. My mother was most impressive when demonstrating breathing from the diaphragm because she had an enormous bosom, which would rise several inches when she breathed in, and slowly subside while she breathed out, all the while humming 'Om' for far longer than seemed possible and finishing with 'Pah!' She would urge her pupils to place their hands on her diaphragm while she performed this feat, much to their consternation.

Each lesson began with breathing – humming *Om* and shouting *Pah* – followed by vowel exercises such as 'Behold he sold the old rolled gold bowl', which was where the real war against Common was waged. Then there were the tongue twisters – An anemone, my enemy; Unique New York; Red lorry, yellow lorry; Selfish shellfish; The sixth sick sheik's sixth sheep's sick, Six thick thistle sticks, six thick thistles stick; The Leith police dismisseth us, and Three free throws, which I don't think anyone ever said correctly, even my mother. Then there was the dangerous pheasant plucker who could so easily lead one astray:

> I am not the pheasant plucker,
> I am the pheasant plucker's mate.
> I am only plucking pheasants
> 'Cos the pheasant plucker's late.

And finally the exercise in consonant definition which had to be shouted while marching round the room and swinging one's arms:

> Zinty tinty tuppenny bun!
> The fox went out to have some fun!
> He had some fun!
> He banged the drum!
> Zinty tinty tuppenny bun!

This was the daily Muzak of my life from the age of eight, when we moved to Twickenham, to fourteen, when my mother stopped working from home and became a school-teacher. My mother would already have a pupil in her studio when I came back from school, and I could pretty well tell the time from whether they were at the Om and Pah stage or beholding their old rolled gold bowls. I would let myself in as quietly as possible, ignoring any pupils who were waiting in the hall, make myself a cup of tea and settle in the breakfast room to do my homework. But through the wall I could always hear the Oms and Pahs and then the ghastly moment when they started on their 'set pieces', which they had to learn for exams and competitions. How well I knew them all!

> Dirty British steamer with a salt-caked smoke stack
> Butting through the Channel in a mad March haze
> With a cargo of Tyne coal, road rails, pig lead
> Firewood, ironware and cheap tin trays.
> (John Masefield, 'Cargoes')

Up the airy mountain
Down the rushy glen
We daren't go a-hunting
For fear of little men.
(William Allingham, 'The Fairies')

Do you remember an Inn, Miranda?
Do you remember an Inn?
And the tedding and the spreading
Of the straw for a bedding
And the fleas that tease in the High Pyrenees
And the wine that tasted of the tar?
And the cheers and the jeers of the young muleteers
(Under the vine of the dark verandah?)
Do you remember an Inn, Miranda?
Do you remember an Inn?
(Hilaire Belloc, 'Tarantella')

Years later, when I read Eng Lit at Oxford, I learned many much better poems by heart – Shakespeare's sonnets, Keats' odes, miles of Yeats – but if you held a gun to my head today and said 'Recite a poem', it would almost certainly be 'Cargoes' or 'Do you remember an Inn, Miranda?' These are still the poems that flash into my mind unbidden – *unwanted!* – at odd moments of the day. '*Dirty* British steamer with a salt-caked smokestack,' I mutter, crashing my trolley along the Waitrose aisles. 'Is there anybody there, said the Traveller' as I wait for the call centre to answer.

It occurs to me that most of the poems my mother taught would have seemed 'modern' at the time, or modernist, in that they derived more from Browning than Wordsworth. But then, if they were modern, why were they so obsessed with goblins and elves? Where did *that* come from? Was there some elvish revival, perhaps associated with the Celtic revival, in the early decades of the twentieth century? And of course as soon as I write elvish, I think, Oh yes, Tolkein, and remember that there was also a folk revival, associated with Morris dancing and Cecil Sharp, in the Thirties, which must have played a part. But still, they were bloody irritating, those elves.

For elocution competitions and exams, it wasn't enough just to *recite* a poem – all the words had to be accompanied by gestures. Thus, references to moonlight, sunlight, stars or any form of weather involved looking upwards; references to storms, rain, frost, involved pulling an imaginary shawl round one's shoulders and blowing on one's nails. (Does anyone, in real life, ever blow on their nails? I have never seen it.) Weeping or even mild regret meant wiping one's eyes with the back of one's hand; laughing meant much shaking of the shoulders, à la Edward Heath. Elves and fairies always started their speeches in a crouching position and then leapt up, spun round, and dashed madly across the stage with arms outstretched. Skipping was sometimes required. Searching for anything or even just looking necessitated a hand above the eyebrows shielding the eyes, accompanied by a pointing gesture. All this activity was tiring and of course baffling, but as nothing compared to the contortions of duologue. Duologue – as opposed to dialogue, which entailed two players – was a curious invention peculiar, I imagine, to elocution lessons. It involved playing two people (if you were lucky – unfortunately it more often entailed one person plus elf) which demanded incredible agility because you had to make a half turn every time the speaker changed and if possible a height change too – one speaker would crouch – and adopt a different accent, or at least timbre, to differentiate the speakers.

There was a particularly horrible piece called 'Overheard on a Salmarsh' (*sic* – though presumably he meant saltmarsh) by Harold Munro which went as follows:

> Nymph, nymph, what are your beads?
> Green glass, goblin. Why do you stare at them?
> Give them me.
> No.
> Give them me. Give them me.
> No.
> Then I will howl all night in the reeds,
> Lie in the mud and howl for them.
> Goblin, why do you love them so? Etc etc.

Nymph for some reason always stood on tiptoe, with arms stretched backwards at 45 degrees to suggest wings, while goblin squatted with one arm over his head denoting (I think) ugliness or physical deformity. He had a deep gruff voice whereas nymph spoke in a high flutey voice like our new Queen Elizabeth. The aim was to be able to switch voices and postures at speed, presumably

16

before the audience dropped off with boredom. I was always so keen to get onto the next line I would be spinning, turning, crouching, like a demented acrobat, while muttering to myself and counting the seconds till it would all be over.

The most dreadful of all the set pieces was a passage from 'Goblin Market' by Christina Rossetti which required positively dervish-like movements, viz:

> Laughed every goblin
> When they spied her peeping:
> Came towards her hobbling,
> Flying, running, leaping,
> Puffing and blowing,
> Chuckling, clapping, crowing,
> Clucking and gobbling,
> Mopping and mowing,
> Full of airs and graces,
> Pulling wry faces,
> Demure grimaces,
> Cat-like and rat-like,
> Ratel- and wombat-like,
> Snail-paced in a hurry. *Et bloody cetera.*

I mean what, for godsake, is a ratel, and how do you pull a demure grimace or achieve 'snail-paced in a hurry'?

Of course it was my mother's dearest wish that I should fulfil her own lost dream and become an actress, so she started me on the zinty-tintys almost as soon as I could speak. By nine or ten, I was a veteran of LAMDA exams

17

and poetry-reading festivals. Almost every Saturday my mother and I would set off to some faraway suburb (Wimbledon, or Surbiton, or Bromley) to spend the afternoon in an echoing hall listening to children recite 'Up the airy mountain'. I was outwardly compliant but my body betrayed my inner rebellion: on the morning of any major competition I was guaranteed to wake with a golf-ball-sized stye on my eye. These styes were invariably blamed for my failure to win gold medals – I sometimes won bronze, and always came away with a certificate saying Commended, but I think everyone got those.

To make matters worse, my mother had a pupil called Lynn Hope who was the same age as me. Our mothers fondly referred to us as 'the two Lynns' and told other people that we were best friends though the most cursory observation would have shown that we loathed each other. I regarded Lynn Hope as hopelessly thick; she no doubt regarded me as stuck up, which I was. But because we were the same age, we were entered in the same competitions, where Lynn Hope would always win a gold medal to my silver or bronze to my Commended. With her foghorn voice and unshakeable confidence, her nauseating dimples, white frilly socks, black patent shoes, and yukky habit of clapping her hands excitedly and saying 'Oh I can't *believe* it!' every time she won, she was the Shirley Temple of the Middlesex poetry-festival circuit. And every time she won, there was a ghastly charade when my mother would rush over to Lynn Hope and hug her, and Lynn would cry 'Oh thank you, thank you, Mrs Barber!' and they would hold hands and do a little bow to the audience, whereby my mother asserted ownership of this prize pupil, and I would skulk and glower behind my golf-ball stye. I once overheard another elocution teacher saying, 'It must be so sad for Mrs Barber that her daughter never wins.' Once or twice, I noticed, my mother contrived to put me in for competitions without entering Lynn Hope. But even then I didn't win, and my mother would have to invent ever more fantastic excuses for my infallible failure.

I realised quite early on that this upset my mother far more than it did me. She really had set her heart on my becoming an actress. And she had a whole litany of hopeful projections to keep the dream alive – 'when you are older', 'when your voice deepens', 'when you fill out' (I was still skeletally thin in those days), *then* I would emerge as the shining thespian I was surely meant to be. But the great difference between my mother and me, then as now, was that I had no aptitude for self-delusion. Even at seven or eight, sulking through those interminable poetry readings, listening to the tenth and twelfth renditions of 'Your green glass beads on a silver ring', I could see that there were other children who were simply better than me. They were clearer, louder, bolder, altogether more dramatic. They skipped onto the stage where I plodded; they beamed at the audience where I scowled; they were prettier, winsomer, charminger and quite frankly more talented. Sometimes I even felt a twinge of admiration.

When I started secondary school, I managed to persuade my mother that I no longer had time to enter poetry competitions – and anyway, I think by then even she was discouraged. But she would not give up all her dreams for me. Instead, she wrote to the BBC to ask them to give me an audition. I had prepared a scene from *Androcles and the Lion*, or was it *The Boy with a Cart*? – some unspeakable bilge anyway – and at the end the producer said thank you, in a way which I knew betokened no thanks. But then he asked me to do some sight reading and, rather to my horror, gave me top marks. The upshot was that I was sent to *Children's Hour*, to read children's letters under 'Uncle' Adrian Thomas. This was good fun, in fact a complete doddle. Every few weeks I would have an afternoon off school to go to Broadcasting House where, with three other children, we would spend an hour in a basement studio reading out letters from listeners. There were always four readers, two boys and two girls, of which one would take the letters from younger listeners and one from older. This was fine when I started – I was eleven or twelve and although it was demeaning to have to read illiterate drivel from six- and seven-year-olds, I was always delighted with the cheque and the afternoon off school, and confidently looked forward to graduating to 'senior girl' eventually.

Then came the day when Jane Asher arrived. I was by this time fourteen, Asher was two or three years younger, but alarmingly poised and pretty. The producer said they just wanted to check sound levels and gave Jane a letter to read, and me another letter. Then, after some muttered conferring, they gave me and Jane a pile of letters each and told us – as usual – to go into the green room and practise reading them. But what was this! My pile was still full of idiot scrawls from six-year-olds, whereas Jane was reading stuff from teenagers! How could this be? 'There must be some mistake,' I said to the producer, 'I'm senior girl! I'm older than her!' 'Yes,' she said sweetly, 'but your voice sounds younger than Jane's.' 'No!' I cried. 'It's not fair. I won't do it!' I threw a full-blown tantrum, complete with tears and shouting. They calmed me down and somehow got me through the broadcast. But I was never asked to read letters on *Children's Hour* again.

That was the end of my elocution career. But alas, I am left with this terrible legacy – my accent. It is the classic elocution accent, homeless and inauthentic, suggestive neither of grouse moor nor shop floor, an accent that screams 'phoney!' the moment it opens its mouth. It is by far the most repulsive thing about me, and I notice that people meeting me for the first time are often taken aback. I have no idea what my natural accent should be – my father still speaks broad Lancashire, my mother elocution. But perhaps it was because I so hated my voice that I chose to become a writer. By thirteen or fourteen, I was writing regular children's columns for the *Richmond and Twickenham Times* and being paid for them. And that was something I arranged entirely by myself, with no help from my mother. I felt, as Julie Burchill memorably remarked, that when I discovered writing it was as if I'd been speaking a second language up till then and had finally found my mother tongue.

An Education

By the time I was sixteen, I had 'filled out' as my mother always promised I would, and, with my new curves and hair no longer in plaits, was beginning to become quite a looker. Also, I'd swept the board at O-level and was well on track to do English, French, Latin at A-level and go on to Oxford. The only fear was that my Latin would 'let me down' – in those days you had to have A-level Latin if you wanted to read English at Oxford – a fact that still makes me go white with fury. I could probably speak four languages now if I hadn't had to waste all those years learning Latin.

Meanwhile, my mother had stopped giving elocution lessons and become a proper schoolteacher. It started when Twickenham County Girls' School over the road asked if she could give occasional elocution and drama classes, which she did, and then asked her to fill in for an absent English teacher. In no time at all she was a full-time English teacher and then head of English. I always found it shocking that she could be head of English while privately preferring Georgette Heyer to Jane Austen, and Walter de la Mare to Wordsworth, and occasionally thought of writing to the education authorities to denounce her. It was only because I didn't, I felt, that she was able to continue her remorseless rise up the educational hierarchy. But anyway she rose so successfully that she ended her career as deputy head of a sixth-form college.

My father also kept getting promoted so we must have been quite well off, but we were never allowed to feel it because my father could never shake off his desperate childhood fear of poverty, and was eternally saving for 'a rainy day'. (In the exceptionally wet winter of 2000, when their house was flooded to a depth of six inches, I cheerily remarked to my father, 'Well it looks like your rainy day has finally come.' Despite his being blind by this stage, in his mid-eighties, and handicapped by water lapping round his ankles, he still tried to wade across the room to hit me.) His great fear was 'fecklessness', which seemed to mean any form of fun. Thus – why did I want to have a Christmas tree? Terrible waste of time, money, all those pine needles buggering the vacuum cleaner and ruining the carpet. 'For fun,' I told him, and watched him almost die of apoplexy on the spot. He regarded any form of social life as time-wasting – to him, my mother's involvement in amateur dramatics was dangerously profligate. But this must have been one of the very few subjects on which she 'dug her heels in', and when my mother dug her heels in, my father knew to retreat.

All my rows were with my father – I remember my early teens as one long row with my father, usually about trivia like what time I went to bed. My mother was a passive, occasionally tearful, spectator. Sometimes when he hit me ('What you need is a clip around the ear') she would intervene, and often after a particularly loud shouting match, when I had stormed up to my room, she would come sidling up with a hot drink and biscuit as a peace offering. 'Can't you be more tactful?' she would urge: 'Why do you *have* to enrage him?' But I despised her peace-making, always too little and too late, and once told her, 'Look, Mum, if you're really on my side, you'll divorce him; otherwise shut up.' So she shut up.

And then Simon entered our lives and everything changed. I met him when I was sixteen and he was – he said twenty-seven, but probably in his late thirties. I was waiting for a bus home to Twickenham after a rehearsal at Richmond Little Theatre (I still consented to appear in my mother's am-dram productions), when a sleek maroon car drew up and a man with a big cigar in his mouth leaned over to the passenger window and said, 'Want a lift?' Of course my parents had told me, my teachers had told me, everyone had told me, never to accept lifts from strange men, but at that stage he didn't seem strange, and I hopped in. I liked the smell of his cigar and the leather seats. He asked where I wanted to go and I said Clifden Road, and he said fine. I told him I had never seen a car like this before, and he said it was a Bristol, and very few were made. He told me lots of facts about Bristols as we cruised – Bristols always cruised – towards Twickenham.

He had a funny accent – later, when I knew him better, I realised it was the accent he used for posh – and I asked if he was foreign. He said, 'Only if you count Jews as foreign.' Well of course I did. I had never consciously met a Jew; I didn't think we had them at my school. But I said politely, 'Are you Jewish? I never would have guessed.' (I meant he didn't have the hooked nose, the greasy ringlets, the straggly beard of Shylock in the school play.) He said he had fought in the Israeli army when he was 'your age'. I wondered what he thought my age was: I hoped he thought nineteen. But then when he said, 'Fancy a coffee?' I foolishly answered, 'No, I have to be home by ten – my father will kill me if I'm late.' 'School tomorrow?' he asked lightly, and, speechless with fury at myself, I could only nod. So then he drove me to my house, and said 'Can I take you out for coffee another evening?'

My life might have turned out differently if I had just said no. But I was not quite rude enough. Instead, I said I was very busy rehearsing a play which meant that unfortunately I had no free evenings. He asked what play, and I said *The Lady's Not for Burning* at Richmond Little Theatre. Arriving for the first night a couple of weeks later, I found an enormous bouquet in the dressing room addressed to me. The other actresses, all grown-ups, were mewing with envy and saying, 'Those flowers must have cost a fortune.' When I left the theatre, hours later, I saw the Bristol parked outside and went over to say thank you. He said 'Can't we have our coffee now?' and I said no, because I was late again, but he could drive me home. I wasn't exactly rushing headlong into this relationship; he was far too old for me to think of him as a boyfriend. On the other hand, I had always fantasised about having an older man, someone even more sophisticated than me, to impress the little squirts of Hampton Grammar. So I agreed to go out with him on Friday week, though I warned that he would have to undergo a grilling from my father.

My father's grillings were <u>notorious</u> among the Hampton Grammar boys. He wanted to know what marks they got at O-level, what A-levels they were taking, what universities they were applying to. He practically made them sit an IQ test before they could take me to the flicks. But this time, for once, my father made no fuss at all. He asked where Simon and I had met; I said at Richmond Little Theatre, and that was that. He seemed <u>genuinely</u> impressed by Simon, and even volunteered that we could stay out till midnight, an hour after my normal weekend curfew. So our meeting for coffee turned into dinner, and with my father's blessing.

Simon took me to an Italian place on Marylebone High Street and of course I was dazzled. I had never been to a proper restaurant before, only to tea rooms with my parents. I didn't understand the menu, but I loved the big pepper grinders and the heavy cutlery, the crêpes Suzette and the champagne. I was also dazzled by Simon's conversation. Again, I understood very little of it, partly because his accent was so strange, but also because it ranged across places and activities I could hardly imagine. My knowledge of the world was based on Shakespeare, Jane Austen, George Eliot and the Brontës and none of them had a word to say about living on a kibbutz or making Molotov cocktails. I felt I had nothing to bring to the conversational feast and blushed when Simon urged me to tell him about my schoolfriends, my teachers, my prize-winning essays. I didn't realise then that my being a schoolgirl was a large part of my attraction.

Over the next few weeks, it became an accepted thing

26

that Simon would turn up on Friday or Saturday nights to take me to 'the West End'. Sometimes we went to the Chelsea Classic to see foreign films; sometimes he took me to concerts at the Wigmore or Royal Festival Hall, but mostly we went to restaurants. The choice of restaurants seemed to be dictated by mysterious visits Simon had to make on the way. He would say 'I've just got to pop into Prince's Gate', and would disappear into one of the white cliff-like houses while I would wait in the car. Sometimes the waiting was very long, and I learned to take a book on all our dates. Once, I asked if I could come in with him, but he said 'No, this is business' and I never asked again.

Besides taking me out at weekends, Simon would sometimes drop in during the week when he said he was 'just passing'. (Why was he passing Twickenham? Where was he going? I never asked.) On these occasions, he would stay chatting to my parents, sometimes for an hour or more, about news or politics – subjects of no interest to me. Often the three of them were so busy talking they didn't even notice if I left the room. I found this extraordinary. It was quite unprecedented in our house for me not to be the centre of attention.

In theory, Simon represented everything my parents most feared – he was not one of us, he was Jewish and cosmopolitan, practically a foreigner! He wore cashmere sweaters and suede shoes; he drove a pointlessly expensive car; he didn't go to work in an office; he was vague about where he went to school and, worst of all, boasted that he had been educated in 'the university of life' – not

27

a teaching establishment my parents recognised. And yet, inexplicably, they liked him. In fact, they liked him more than I ever liked him, perhaps because he took great pains to make them like him. He brought my mother flowers and my father wine; he taught them to play backgammon; he chatted to them endlessly and seemed genuinely interested in their views. I suppose it made a change for them from always talking about me.

Yet none of us ever really knew a thing about him. I think my parents once asked where he lived and he said 'South Kensington' but that was it. I never had a phone number for him, still less an address. As for what he did, he was 'a property developer' – a term that I suspect meant as little to my parents as it did to me. I knew it was somehow connected with these visits he had to make, the great bunches of keys he carried, the piles of surveyors' reports and auction catalogues in the back of his car, and the occasional evenings when he had to 'meet Perec', which meant cruising around Bayswater looking for Perec Rachman's Roller parked outside one of his clubs. Rachman would later give his name to Rachmanism, when the press exposed him as the worst of London's exploitative landlords, but at that time he was just one of Simon's many mysterious business colleagues.

Simon was adept at not answering questions, but actually he rarely needed to, because I never asked them. The extent to which I never asked him questions is astonishing in retrospect – I blame Albert Camus. My normal instinct was to bombard people with questions, to ask about every detail of their lives, even to intrude into their silences with 'What are you thinking?' But just around the time I met Simon I became an Existentialist, and one of the rules of Existentialism as practised by me and my disciples at Lady Eleanor Holles School was that you never asked questions. Asking questions showed that you were naïve and bourgeois; not asking questions showed that you were sophisticated and French. I badly wanted to be sophisticated. And, as it happened, this suited Simon fine. My role in the relationship was to be the schoolgirl ice maiden: implacable, ungrateful, unresponsive to everything he said or did. To ask questions would have shown that I was interested in him, even that I cared, and neither of us really wanted that.

Simon established early on that I was a virgin, and seemed quite happy about it. He asked when I intended to lose my virginity and I said 'Seventeen', and he agreed that was the ideal age. He said it was important not to lose my virginity in some inept fumble with a grubby schoolboy, but with a sophisticated older man. I heartily agreed – though, unlike him, I had no particular older man in mind. He certainly didn't seem like a groper. I was used to Hampton Grammar boys who turned into octopuses in the cinema dark, clamping damp tentacles to your breast. Simon never did that. Instead, he kissed me long and gently and said, 'I love to look into your eyes.' When he kissed me, he called me Minn and said I was to call him Bubl but I usually forgot. Eventually, one night, he said 'I'd love to see your breasts' so I grudgingly unbuttoned my blouse and allowed him to peep inside my bra. But this was still well within the Lady Eleanor Holles dating code – by rights, given the number of hot dinners he'd bought me, he could really have taken my bra right off.

And then my parents threw me into bed with him. One day, on one of his drop-in visits, Simon said he was going to Wales next weekend to visit some friends and could I go with him? I confidently expected my parents to say no – to go *away*, overnight, with a man I barely knew? – but instead they said yes, though my father added jocularly, 'Separate rooms of course.' 'Of course,' said Simon. So off we went for the first of many dirty weekends. I hated Wales, hated the grim hotel, the sour looks when Simon signed us in. We shared a room, of course, and shared a bed, but Simon only kissed me and said, 'Save it till you're seventeen.' After that, there were many more weekends – Paris, Amsterdam, Bruges, and often Sark in the Channel Islands, because Simon liked the hotel there, and I liked stocking up on duty-free Je Reviens and my exciting new discovery, Sobranie Black Russian cigarettes. They brought my sophistication on by leaps and bounds.

As my seventeenth birthday approached, I knew that my debt of dinners and weekends could only be erased by 'giving' Simon my virginity. He talked for weeks beforehand about when, where, how it should be achieved. He thought Rome, or maybe Venice; I thought as near as possible to Twickenham, in case I bled. In the end, it was a new trendy circular hotel – the Ariel? – by Heathrow airport, where we spent the night before an early-morning flight to somewhere or other, I forget. He wanted to do a practice run with a banana – he had brought a banana specially. I said 'Oh for heaven's sake!' and told him to do it properly. He talked a lot about how he hoped Minn would do Bubl the honour of welcoming him into her home. Somewhere in the middle of the talking, he was inside me, and it was over. I thought, 'Oh well, that was easy. Perhaps now I can get a proper boyfriend.'

(I think the word that best describes my entire sex life with Simon is negligible. I never experienced even a glimmer of an orgasm while I was with him. He was a far from ardent lover – he seemed to enjoy waffling about Minn and Bubl more than actually doing anything. And whereas my games mistress was always bellowing across the changing room 'But you said it was your period *last* week!', Simon always took my word for it when I said that Minn was 'indisposed'. So although I spent many nights in bed with Simon, often in foreign hotel rooms, very little ever happened.)

The affair – if it was an affair – drifted on, partly because no proper boyfriends showed up, partly because I had become used to my strange double life of schoolgirl swot during the week, restaurant-going, foreign-travelling sophisticate at weekends. And this life had alienated me from my schoolfriends – if they said 'Are you coming to Eel Pie Jazz Club on Saturday?' I would say 'No, I'm going to Paris with Simon.' Of course my friends all clamoured to meet Simon but I never let them. I was afraid of something – afraid perhaps that they would 'see through him', see, not the James Bond figure I had described, but this rather short, rather ugly, long-faced, splay-footed man who talked in different accents and lied about his age, whose stories didn't add up.

31

Because by now – a year into the relationship – I realised that there was a lot I didn't know about Simon. I knew his cars (he had several Bristols), and the restaurants and clubs he frequented, but I still didn't know where he lived. He took me to a succession of flats which he said were his, but often they were full of gonks and women's clothes and he didn't know where the light switches were. So these were other people's flats, or sometimes empty flats, in Bayswater, South Kensington, Gloucester Road. He seemed to have a limitless supply of them.

Where did I imagine he lived? Incredible as it seems now – but this is a reminder of how young I was – I imagined that he lived with his parents but was ashamed to tell me. I pictured this ancient couple in some East End slum performing strange rituals in Yiddish. The fact that he told me his parents were well off and lived in Cricklewood was neither here nor there: I preferred my version. I suspect this is always the way with conmen: they don't even have to construct a whole story, their victims fill in the gaps, reconcile the irreconcilables – their victims do most of the work. Simon hardly had to con me at all, because I was so busy conning myself.

But by now there was a compelling reason for staying with Simon – I was in love. Not with Simon, obviously, but with his business partner Danny and his girlfriend Helen. I loved them both equally. I loved their beauty, I loved their airy flat in Bedford Square where there were Pre-Raphaelites on the walls and harpsichord music on the hi-fi. At that time, few people in Britain admired the Pre-Raphaelites but Danny was one of the first, and I eagerly followed. He lent me books on Rossetti and Burne-Jones and Millais, and sometimes flattered me by showing me illustrations in auction catalogues and saying 'What do you think? Should I make a bid?' I found it easy to talk to Danny; I could chatter away to him, whereas with Simon I only sulked.

Helen was a different matter. She drifted around silently, exquisitely, a soulful Burne-Jones damsel half-hidden in her cloud of red-gold hair. At first, I was so much in awe of her beauty I could barely speak to her. But gradually I came to realise that her silence was often a cover for not knowing what to say and that actually – I hardly liked to use the word about my goddess – she was thick. I was terrified that one day Danny would find out. And there were sometimes hints from Simon that Danny's interest in Helen might be waning, that there could be other girlfriends. Knowing this, keeping this secret, made me feel that it was crucial for me to go on seeing Helen, to protect her, because one day, when I was just a little older and more sophisticated, we could be best friends.

Simon always refused to talk about business to me ('Oh, you don't want to know about that, Minn') but Danny had no such inhibitions. He loved telling me funny stories about the seething world of dodgy property dealers – the scams, the auction rings, the way the auctioneers sometimes tried to keep out the 'Stamford Hill cowboys' by holding auctions on Yom Kippur or other holy days, and then the sight of all these Hasidic Jews in mufflers and dark glasses trying to bid without being seen. Or the great scam whereby they sold Judah Binstock a quarter acre of Ealing Common, without him realising that the quarter acre was only two yards wide. Through Danny, I learned how Perec Rachman had seemingly solved the problem of 'stats' – statutory or sitting tenants – who were the bane of Sixties property developers. The law gave them the right to stay in their flats at a fixed rent for life if they wanted – and they had a habit of living an awfully long time. But Rachman had certain robust methods, such as carrying out building works all round them, or taking the roof off, or 'putting in the schwartzes' (West Indians) or filling the rest of the house with prostitutes, that made stats eager to move.

So I gathered from Danny that the property business in which Simon was involved was not entirely honest. But my first hint of other forms of dishonesty came about fifteen months into the relationship when I went to a bookshop on Richmond Green. Simon had taken me there several times to buy me books on Jewish history and the works of Isaac Bashevis Singer – I accepted them gratefully, though I never read them. But on this occasion, I went alone and the bookdealer, who was normally so friendly, said 'Where's your friend?'

'What friend?'

'Simon Prewalski.'

'I don't know anyone of that name,' I said truthfully.

'Well, whatever he calls himself. Tell him I'm fed up with his bouncing cheques – I've reported him to the police.'

That evening I said to Simon, 'Do you know anyone called Prewalski?'

'Yes – my mother, my grandparents. Why?'

I told him what the book dealer had said.

Simon said, 'Well, don't go in there again. Or if you do, don't tell him you've seen me. Say we've broken up.'

'But what did he mean about the bouncing cheques?'

'How should I know? Don't worry about it.'

So that was a hint, or more than a hint. But then in Cambridge there was unmistakable proof. He and Danny had gone into Cambridge in a big way and were buying up a street called Bateman Street, so we often stayed there. One weekend I was moaning – I was always moaning – 'I'm bored with Bateman Street' and Danny said, 'So am I – let's drive to the country', so we drove out towards Newmarket. At a place called Six Mile Bottom, I saw a thatched cottage with a For Sale sign outside. 'Look, how pretty,' I said. 'Why can't you two buy nice places like that instead of horrible old slums?' 'Perhaps we can,' said Simon, sliding the Bristol to a stop – 'Fancy it, Danny?' 'Why not?' So Simon parked the car and we all marched up to the door. An old lady answered it: 'The agent didn't tell me you were coming.' 'Oh dear, oh dear,' said Danny, 'how very remiss of him.' She must have liked his posh accent, which was so much more convincing than Simon's, because she said, 'Well, come in anyway – I'll show you round.'

The cottage was full, over-full, of antique furniture: I found it gloomy and was bored within minutes. But Simon and Danny both seemed enchanted and kept admiring the beams, the polished floorboards, the pictures, the furniture. Having been rather crabby, the owner blossomed into friendliness and invited us to stay for coffee. While she was making it, Simon asked if he could go upstairs to the bathroom. A few minutes later I saw him going out to the car carrying something. Then he joined us for coffee and, after half an hour chatting, we left. In the car, Danny said, 'Got it?'

Simon nodded.

'Speed?'

'Pretty sure.'

'Got what?' I said.

'So was that your dream cottage?' said Danny. 'Will you and Simon live there happily ever after?'

'No.' I said. 'I found it gloomy.'

They both laughed. 'You're so difficult to please.'

Danny said he must get back to Bateman Street. I was still furious with him and Simon for laughing at me, so I said, 'You promised me a day in the country – I'm not going back.' Danny said we could drop him in Newmarket so we took him to the station, then went to a hotel for lunch. We were having a rather lugubrious meal when two men came into the dining room and one pointed the other towards our table. The man introduced himself as a detective. He said, 'We've had a complaint from a Mrs so-and-so of Six Mile Bottom. She says two men and a girl visited her cottage this morning and afterwards she noticed that a valuable antique map by Speed was missing from one of the bedrooms.' 'Oh, *Simon*!' I said. He shot me a look. 'Perhaps we could have this conversation outside,' he suggested. He went outside with the policeman. I waited a few minutes and then went to the Ladies, and from the Ladies walked out the back door and away down the street. I had just enough money for a bus to Cambridge, and ran panting to find Danny in Bateman Street. 'Simon's been arrested!' I told him. 'He stole a map from that old lady!'

'I'm sure there was a misunderstanding,' he said smoothly. 'I'll sort it out. Why don't you take the train back to London?'

'I don't have any money!' I wailed.

He handed me a £10 note. 'Don't worry about Simon,' he told me. I didn't intend to: I hoped he was in prison.

He wasn't, of course; he bounced round to Clifden Road a few days later and took me out to dinner. 'How could you *steal* from an old lady?'

'I didn't steal. She asked me to have the map valued.'

'No she didn't, I was with you.'

'All right, she didn't ask me. But I recognised that the map was by Speed and thought if I got it valued for her, it would be a nice surprise.'

I knew he was lying, but I let it go. I said: 'If you ever really stole something, I would leave you.'

He said, 'I know you would, Minn.'

But actually I knew he had stolen something and I didn't leave him, so we were both lying.

Soon afterwards, I did try to leave him. I was bored. I was bored with Minn and Bubl, with the endless driving round, the waiting while he ran his mysterious errands, the long heavy meals in restaurants, the tussles in strange bedrooms, the fact that we never met anyone except

Danny and Helen. I loved the evenings in Bedford Square when Danny played the harpsichord and Helen showed me her new clothes, but now they spent most of their time in Cambridge and Simon was never going to Cambridge again. I told Simon, 'We're finished – I've got to concentrate on my A-levels.' He said, 'We're not finished. I'll come for you when you've done your A-levels.'

On the evening I finished sitting my A-levels, Simon took me out to dinner and proposed. I had wanted him to propose, as proof of my power, but I had absolutely no intention of accepting because of course I was going to Oxford. Eighteen years of my life had been dedicated to this end, so it was quite impertinent of him to suggest my giving it up. I relayed the news to my parents the next morning as a great joke – 'Guess what? Simon proposed! He wants me to marry him this summer!' To my complete disbelief, my father said 'Why not?' *Why not*? Had he suddenly gone demented? 'Because then I couldn't go to Oxford.' My father said, 'Well, is that the end of the world? Look,' he went on, 'You've been going out with him for two years; he's obviously serious, he's a good man; don't mess him around.' I turned to my mother incredulously but she shook her head. 'You don't need to go to university if you've got a good husband.'

This was 1962, well before the advent of feminism. But even so, I felt a sense of utter betrayal, as if I'd spent eighteen years in a convent and then the Mother Superior had said, 'Of course, you know, God doesn't exist.' I couldn't believe my parents could abandon the idea of Oxford. But apparently they could and over the next few days they

38

argued it every mealtime – good husbands don't grow on trees, you're lucky to get this one ('And you not even in the family way!'), why go to university if you don't need to? Simon meanwhile was taking me to see houses, asking where I wanted to live when we were married. I couldn't resist telling my schoolfriends, 'I'm engaged!' And they were all wildly excited and thrilled for me and said, 'You'll never have to do Latin again!' Even so, I was queasy – I'd always liked the sound of Oxford, I even liked writing essays, I wasn't so keen to give up the idea. But my parents, especially my father, put great pressure on me. Why go to Oxford if I could marry Simon? And, they reminded me, I'd been saying all along that I couldn't face another term at school.

This was true. In those days, if you were aiming for Oxford or Cambridge, you had to stay at school an extra term after A-levels to prepare for the entrance exams. I was dreading it because Miss R. Garwood Scott, the headmistress, had flatly refused to make me a prefect and, while all the other Oxbridge candidates could spend their time in the prefects' room, I would be left roaming the corridors or slouching round the playing field on my own, without any gang to protect me. But Miss R. Garwood Scott was adamant that I would never be a prefect even if I stayed at school a hundred years – I was a troublemaker, a bad influence, guilty of dumb insolence and making pupils laugh at teachers. I put a brave face on it, but I knew the next term was going to be the loneliest three months of my life. But then there was the glittering prize of Oxford at the end of it – I never doubted I would get in – and I had resolved it was a price I was willing to pay.

Events overtook me in the last few days of term. Miss R. Garwood Scott somehow got wind of my engagement and summoned me to see her. Was it true I was engaged? Yes, I said, but I would still like to take the Oxford exams. She was ruthless. I could either be engaged or take the exams but not both. When was the wedding and which church would it be in? Not in church, I said, because my fiancé was Jewish. Jewish! She looked aghast – 'Don't you realise that the Jews killed Our Lord?' I stared at her. 'So I won't take the Oxford exams,' I said. My little gang was waiting for me outside her study. 'I told her I was leaving,' I announced. 'She tried to persuade me to stay but I refused.' They all congratulated me and begged to be bridesmaids. Then I went to the bogs and cried my eyes out.

I told my parents: 'I'm not going to Oxford, I'm marrying Simon.' 'Oh good!' they said. 'Wonderful.' When Simon came that evening, they made lots of happy jokes about not losing a daughter but gaining a son. Simon chuckled and waved his hands about, poured drinks and proposed toasts – but I caught the flash of panic in his eyes. A few days later, probably no more than a week, we were in the Bristol on our way to dinner when he said he just needed to pop into one of his flats to have a word with a tenant. Fine, I said, I'll wait in the car. As soon as he went inside the house, I opened the glove compartment and started going through the letters and bills he kept in there. It was something I could have done on any one of a hundred occasions before – I knew he kept correspondence in the glove compartment, I knew the glove compartment was unlocked, I was often waiting in the car alone and had no scruples about reading other people's letters. So why had I never done it before? And why did it seem the most obvious thing in the world to do now? Anyway, the result was instantaneous. There were a dozen or more letters addressed to Simon Goldman, with a Twickenham address. And two addressed to Mr and Mrs Simon Goldman with the same address.

I behaved quite normally that evening though at the end, when he asked if Minn would welcome a visit from Bubl, I replied smoothly that she was indisposed. By that stage, I was at least as good a liar as Simon. As soon as I got home, I looked in the phone book – and why had I never thought of doing *that* before? – and sure enough found an S. Goldman with a Popes Grove (Twickenham) number, and the address I'd seen on the letters. It was only about half a mile from my house. I actually passed it every day on the bus to school. I spent the night plotting and rehearsing what I would say, working out scripts for all eventualities. When I finally rang the number the next morning, it was all over in seconds. A woman answered. 'Mrs Goldman?' I said. 'Yes.' 'I'm ringing about the Bristol your husband advertised for sale.' 'Oh,' she said, 'is he selling it? He's not here now but he's usually back about six.' That was enough, or more than enough – I could hear a child crying in the background.

I took the train to Waterloo, and walked all the way to Bedford Square. Helen was in, and guessed as soon as she saw me – 'You've found out?'

'Yes,' I said. 'It's not just that he's married – he *lives* with her. And there's a child.'

'Two, actually.'

'Why didn't you tell me?'

'I'm sorry. I wanted to. The other night when you said were engaged, I told Danny we *must* tell you, but he said Simon would never forgive us.'

This was – what? – my third, fourth, fifth betrayal by adults? And I had really thought Helen was my friend.

'What was Simon planning to do?' I asked her. 'Commit bigamy?'

'Yes,' she said soberly. 'That's exactly what he intended to do. He felt he'd lose you if he didn't. He loves you very much, you know.'

I went home and raged at my parents – 'You did this. *You* made me go out with him, *you* made me get engaged.' My parents were white with shock – unlike me, they had no inkling before that Simon was dishonest. My mother cried. When Simon came that evening, my father went to the door and tried to punch him. I heard him shouting, 'You've ruined her life!' From my bedroom window, I saw Simon sitting in the Bristol outside with his shoulders shaking. Then my father strode down the front path and kicked the car as hard as he could, and Simon drove away. I found the sight of my father kicking the car hilarious and wanted to shout out of the window, 'Scratch it, Dad! Scratch the bodywork – that'll *really* upset him!'

It was a strange summer. My parents were grieving and still in deep shock. I, the less deceived, was faking far more sorrow than I felt. After all, I never loved him whereas I think perhaps they did. I stayed in my room playing César Franck's *Symphony in D Minor* very loudly day after day. My main emotion was rage, followed by puzzlement about what to do next. I had no plans for the summer or – now – for the rest of my life. When my A-level results came, I not only got the top marks I fully expected in English and French, but also – *mirabile dictu* – top marks in Latin. I slapped the letter on the breakfast table and said, 'You see? I *could* have gone to Oxford.'

My father took the day off work, probably for the first time in his life, and went to see Miss R. Garwood Scott. God knows what humble pie he had to eat – and he hated humble pie – but he came back with a grim face and a huge concession. She had agreed I could be entered for the Oxford exams as a Lady Eleanor Holles pupil, and I could sit the exams at school. But she was adamant that I could not attend the school – it was up to him to arrange private tutorials. Mum and Dad talked far into the night about how they would find a tutor, and how they would pay. A day or two later – presumably at Miss R. Garwood Scott's instigation – one of my English teachers rang and volunteered to be my tutor. She even offered to teach me for free, though I think my father insisted on paying. So I spent that autumn writing essays and going to tutorials, working hard and feeling lonely. My parents were in such deep grief that mealtimes were silent. Once or twice I saw the Bristol parked at the end of the street, but I was never remotely tempted to go to it.

43

One day that winter, sitting at my bedroom table writing an essay, I saw a woman walking slowly along the street looking at our house. I guessed immediately that she was Simon's wife. She was prettier than I'd imagined her, but of course mumsy and old. A few minutes later she walked back again and came up the path. My mother must have been watching from the downstairs window because she shouted to me, 'Stay in your room', and then fetched the woman in. They talked for about half an hour. My mother wouldn't tell me afterwards what Mrs Goldman had said – with her typical beta-brain logic she said it was none of my business. But she couldn't resist saying, with strange malice, 'You weren't the first, you know. He had other girlfriends before you. Anyway,' she went on, 'he's in prison now – best place for him.' For a moment, I thought she meant he was in prison for having girlfriends, but Mum said no – he'd been caught bouncing cheques. He was charged with three offences, asked for 190 others to be taken into account, and was sentenced to six months.

I sat the Oxford exams, I went for interviews, I was accepted at St Anne's. In my second term at Oxford, one of the nuns who ran my hall of residence handed me a note which she said a man had brought. It said, 'Bubl respectfully requests the pleasure of the company of Minn for dinner at the Randolph Hotel tonight at 8.' I tore it up in front of the nun. 'Don't ever let that man in,' I told her. 'He's a con man.' I went round to Merton to tell my boyfriend Dick and he said, 'Well, I'd like to meet him – let's go to the Randolph.' So we did. Simon was sitting in the lobby – on time, for once in his life – looking older, tireder, seedier than I remembered. His face lit up when he saw me and fell when I said, 'This is my boyfriend, Dick.' Simon said politely, 'Won't you please both stay to dinner as my guests?' 'How are you going to pay for it?' I snapped and Dick looked at me with horror – he had never heard me use that tone before. Simon silently withdrew a large roll of banknotes from his pocket and I nodded, okay.

Dick was enchanted by Simon. He loved his Isracli kibbutz stories, his fishing-with-dynamite stories, his Molotov cocktail stories. I had heard them all before, except his new prison stories, and sulked throughout the meal. Simon said that when he got out of prison, he headed immediately for Sark – and here he cast me such a doe-eyed soppy look I almost spat – but he was re-arrested as soon as he got off the plane in Jersey, because he had passed some dud cheques in the Channel Islands which were not 'taken into account'. As Dick walked me back to my convent, he said, 'I see why you were taken in by him – he is quite a charmer, isn't he?' 'No,' I said furiously, 'he's a disgusting criminal con man and don't you *dare* say you like him!'

Was Simon a con man? Well, he was a liar and a thief who used charm as his jemmy to break into my parents' house and steal their most treasured possession, which was me. Of course Oxford, and time, would have stolen me away eventually, but Simon made it happen almost overnight. Until our 'engagement', I'd thought my parents were ignorant about many things (fashion, for instance, and Existentialism, and why Jane Austen was better than Georgette Heyer) but I accepted their moral authority unquestioningly. So when they casually dropped the educational evangelism they'd sold me for eighteen years and told me I should skip Oxford to marry Simon, I thought, 'I'm never going to take your advice about anything ever again.' And when he turned out to be married, it was as if, tacitly, they concurred. From then on, whenever I told them my plans, their only response was a penitent 'You know best.'

What did I get from Simon? An education – the thing my parents always wanted me to have. I learned a lot in my two years with Simon. I learned about expensive restaurants and luxury hotels and foreign travel, I learned about antiques and Bergman films and classical music. All this was useful when I went to Oxford – I could read a menu, I could recognise a finger bowl, I could follow an opera, I was not a complete hick. But actually there was a much bigger bonus than that. My experience with Simon entirely cured my craving for sophistication. By the time I got to Oxford I wanted nothing more than to meet kind, decent, conventional boys my own age, no matter if they were gauche or virgins. I would marry one eventually and stay married all my life and for that, I suppose, I have Simon to thank.

But there were other lessons Simon taught me that I regret learning. I learned not to trust people; I learned not to believe what they say but to watch what they do; I learned to suspect that anyone and everyone is capable of 'living a lie'. I came to believe that other people – even when you think you know them well – are ultimately unknowable. Learning all this was a good basis for my subsequent career as an interviewer, but not, I think, for life. It made me too wary, too cautious, too ungiving. I was damaged by my education.

Oxford

I did the hardest intellectual work of my life at Oxford, but not studying Eng Lit – it was all to do with trying to become a completely different person to the one I grew up as. The Simon debacle had dealt a huge blow to my confidence. I had felt I knew everything and now realised I knew nothing. More importantly, everything I had learned or assimilated from my parents I now regarded as unreliable, and needing to be rethought from scratch. In fact, I probably went further – I felt that *everything* my parents believed was by definition wrong, and that if I ever found myself in agreement with my parents I should immediately recant. Everything from my father's 'Neither a borrower nor a lender be' to my mother's 'Blue and green should never be seen' needed to be jettisoned. But in a way what they said wasn't the problem: what I was more worried about was the attitudes, prejudices, beliefs I might have picked up from them subconsciously or before I was old enough even to know what I was learning. Effectively, I had to question everything I believed, and never accept my own instincts. It required constant vigilance; it was intellectually exhausting.

My parents never explicitly articulated their belief systems (and my mother's was not quite the same as my father's) but common to both and therefore the view I grew up with was that work was good, pleasure was bad; self-denial was good, self-indulgence was bad; saving money was good, spending it was bad; gambling was unthinkable; fecklessness spelled ruin. People who ignored these rules came to sticky ends. Briefly, I suppose, it was a typical English lower-middle-class puritanism with a strong emphasis on caution, isolationism, 'not interfering', thrift, prudery, moral condemnation and deep fear of the unknown, which included everything from foreigners to unfamiliar vegetables.

On top of this, my mother gave me the weird advice, drummed into me for years, that I must never make friends with 'obvious' people, which meant anyone pretty or popular or even likable; that I must seek out girls with acne or dandruff, with horrible whiney voices and miserable attitudes, because only among them, she said, could I find 'real friends'. The others, the popular and pretty ones, she told me, would betray me. And although I had never particularly – thank God – acted on this advice, it was always somehow there in the back of my mind, making me distrustful of attractive or popular people. And yet if I'd thought about it, even for a minute, I would have seen that my mother was a poor teacher of friendship because she had so few friends herself.

Anyway, it meant that I arrived at Oxford absolutely determined to learn – not Eng Lit, obviously, but how to have fun. The rule from now on would be that I would go to every party I was invited to, flirt with every man I ever met, drink every drink, smoke every joint, never sacrifice a lunch for a lecture, or a party for a tutorial. The gift for

49

fierce concentration that had got me top marks in A-levels would take me through Oxford and out into the world as a fully qualified hedonist and femme fatale. I would study the beautiful people and join their ranks, or at least hang on their coat-tails. Give me public-school captains of cricket, give me dazzling daughters of duchesses, not acne'd cleverclogs from northern grammar schools. I was going to be a good-time-girl, dammit. I was going to work really hard at this pleasure lark. And I would study men, men, men, because I knew I was woefully ignorant in this field. The only two men I'd known so far were Simon and my father and they were both, in their different ways, hopelessly wrong.

And Oxford was the ideal place to study men because in those days there were seven male undergraduates for every one female, and if you were reasonably pretty, as I was, you really had to beat them off like flies. Moreover, most of them were rich or at least had daddies rich enough to send them to public schools – shocking in retrospect, I know, but at the time I was simply happy that there were so many men eager to buy me dinner. I particularly liked the ones with sports cars who could whisk me off to country restaurants like the Rose Revived, or the ones who brought champagne and Fortnum's hampers to take me punting. There was never any question of going Dutch. Presumably there were some poor grammar school boys skulking around the pubs somewhere but I never met them.

I was lucky in that on my very first day at St Anne's I was befriended by a fellow fresher called Maria Aitken, the tall, witty, beautiful daughter of an MP who lived in a moated grange in Suffolk. She was a good mentor for my new life of hedonism. No sooner had I met her than I received an invitation from her brother, Jonathan Aitken, to a meeting of 'The James Bond Society' at the Union. I asked Maria what this meant and she laughed and said, 'Just one of Jonathan's bright ideas' – what it actually meant was Jonathan Aitken in a dinner jacket and about a dozen pretty freshwomen in their best frocks, with waiters serving vodka martinis shaken not stirred. Wotta pillock, I thought. But there were plenty of other invitations from non-pillocks – every day there would be a satisfying little stack of envelopes in my pigeonhole, inviting me to tea, to drinks, to punting picnics, *fêtes champêtres*, cocktail parties. At first I found some of them puzzling – I remember asking Maria why does it say 'At home' when the party is at Magdalen? Maria guided me through these early minefields, and taught me that if an invitation said 'Drinks 6–8' I didn't actually have to arrive on the dot at six and drink solidly till eight – I was meant to arrive about seven and stay no more than an hour. By my second term, I thought I was familiar with all possible party permutations but was baffled by an invitation to a reading party in Devon at Easter. 'What do you do at a reading party?' I asked, puzzled. 'Mm, you stay in a rented cottage and read books.' That was one of the few party invitations I refused.

I wasn't particularly alarmed when I received my first invitation to a dinner party because I assumed it just meant dinner at a restaurant – which I was used to from Simon – but with more people. But this one was at the

Bear in Woodstock and incredibly grand, with about sixteen guests all in black tie, and place cards round the table. I was invited by Charles Vyvyan, a Balliol man who asked me out occasionally – I never knew why because he never seemed remotely interested in me – and I was wearing my usual tarty-party dress which was far too short and low-cut for this company. I didn't know anyone else there and to my dismay was placed far away from Charles, between two very grand dons. One of them was Maurice Keen, who was later rumoured to have been Oxford's main conduit for recruiting spies, though of course I didn't know that then. Having to talk to a don was frightening enough, but then he persisted in asking me ludicrous questions like did I prefer Elizabeth I or Mary, Queen of Scots? I wouldn't know, I told him, I was reading English, not history. Oh. He fell silent for a while and then came back with which character in Dickens would I most like to be? I haven't done Dickens yet, I told him. Oh. Despairingly, he made his third attempt: 'How are you getting on with Lady Ogilvie?' Who is Lady Ogilvie? I asked. Oh, I thought you said you were at St. Anne's? I am. Well I think you'll find that Lady Ogilvie is the Principal of your college. The horror, the horror.

Another horror that first term was finding there were people my own age cleverer than me! This had never happened at Lady Eleanor Holles. There were rumours at school of two science swots and a new girl who was supposed to be a 'genius' at mathematics, but they didn't count. I was Lady Eleanor Holles's undisputed English star and it never occurred to me that every other school in the country would have its own English star and that I would encounter many of them at Oxford. But for my very first tutorial I was assigned a partner, Charlotte B, who I realised within minutes was twice as intelligent as me. The subject was Spenser's *Faerie Queene* and I thought it was pretty heroic of me just to have read a few cantos of the fusty nonsense, but she had evidently read the whole thing and – incredibly – enjoyed it. She and our tutor, Miss Morrison, spent the whole hour enthusiastically exchanging Spenser quotes, while I sulked and panicked.

There was to be a lot of panicking and sulking that first term, especially when it was revealed that we were meant to *teach ourselves* Anglo-Saxon. We were given a grammar book and dictionary and told to just get on with it till we were ready to translate *Beowulf*. I knew I would never be ready to translate *Beowulf* and panicked so hard I actually developed shingles and was sent home with an aegrotat. It meant I avoided the end-of-term exams, and never really learned Anglo-Saxon. That long Christmas at Twickenham gave me time to digest the fact that, by Oxford standards, I was intellectually second-rate. Up till then, I'd always thought I was brilliant – if I ever failed to excel, it was simply because I hadn't done enough work. But tutorials with Charlotte taught me that some people actually had better *brains* than mine and that no amount of swotting would enable me to compete. It was a blow to my pride but not to my hopes – I had never particularly set my heart on getting a first.

But it made for yet another shift from my parents. Cleverness, and academic attainment, were almost the only values they had taught me to aspire to and, as far as they were concerned, I had ticked all the boxes by getting into Oxford. But once I got to Oxford I realised that cleverness was not all it was cracked up to be – that there were other qualities, like sensitivity, like kindness, like charm, like tact, that I had never given a moment's thought to, but that were actually far more important. I didn't quite swing round to Charles Kingsley's view – 'Be good, sweet maid, and let who can be clever' – but I was beginning to think I should pay less attention to being clever and more to being good.

On top of that, the Simon debacle left me with a strong distrust of book learning, which I still to some extent retain. My feeling was: I've read all these books, I'm supposed to be so clever, and yet I couldn't even spot the most obvious con trick in the world. I felt that what I urgently needed to understand was Real Life and that Milton and Spenser were of no possible help. This was a poor attitude for embarking on three years study of English Literature. It meant that I read the classics impatiently, instead of luxuriating in them as I had at school, because I was dying to learn about the present day. I think it was this attitude that propelled me towards journalism – I still have a somewhat exaggerated hatred of anything to do with the past. I must have done *some* work because I got a perfectly respectable upper second degree but essentially the Eng Lit course was wasted on me.

On the other hand, I was very diligent in pursuing my self-set course: the study of men. I went out with as many of them as possible – it was quite normal for me to have lunch with one, tea with another, dinner with a third and then pop into a party to pick up new supplies for the following week. My diary was so crowded with men there was no time for lectures and the only chance of writing essays was when I was locked into my room at night. But often, instead of writing essays, I wrote notes on everything I was discovering about men. I studied them exactly as if they were a new species – notes on appearance, habits, habitat, on the strength of which I would make staggering generalisations. 'Men like to talk about their dogs, but not about their sisters.' 'They all seem to gamble.' 'They like to tell you about the games they played at school and their old schoolteachers.' Such was my insatiable curiosity I spent whole evenings asking men about themselves and never resented their failure to ask me any questions back. And I learned never, ever to talk about work. The worst thing I could possibly say was that I enjoyed writing essays. It was important to appear stupid – which was beginning to come quite naturally. At school, I'd loved showing off my intellectual superiority; at Oxford I learned never to attempt it.

My college, St Anne's, tried to cramp my style by putting me in a residential hall called Springfield St Mary run by nuns. Worse still, they gave me the smallest room in the entire college where there was literally no space to swing a cat, let alone a boy, so I spent all my time in the men's colleges. That first year I mainly lived in Merton because I had a boyfriend there called Dick. I met him in an odd way – I was picked up in the street by a tall, handsome Classics postgraduate called Jo who announced that he was taking me to see his younger brother Dick in Merton. Dick, he explained as we loped along, had just arrived at Oxford like me, but was rather shy and still upset about the recent death of their father, so what he needed was a nice girlfriend. Jo explained that he'd reconnoitred all the first-year undergraduates and decided I was the one. I was somewhat bemused by this approach – not least because I fancied Jo – but as soon as I met Dick I was content. He was tall, handsome, witty, charming, and, although he had rather rubbery thick lips, Jo reassured me by saying that he looked exactly like Jean-Paul Belmondo. Within a day or two, we were officially a couple (though not yet lovers) and walking round Oxford hand in hand.

Dick had only one drawback: he wanted to be an actor (he still is an actor, but under a different name). He had played Henry V at Haileybury and everyone agreed it was the best performance they had ever seen, so he was determined to act in OUDS at Oxford and then conquer the London stage. But it meant that, because we couldn't bear to be parted, I had to go to all these acting auditions where he would be cast as, say, Hamlet and I would be cast as, say, Second Serving Wench. I thought after all my years of elocution lessons and appearing in my mother's am-dram productions I would easily walk into starring roles, but unfortunately at Oxford I was up against actresses who had real talent – Diana Quick for one, Tamara Ustinov for another. Early in my first year, Tamara and I were cast as sisters in a Restoration comedy and I remember looking across the stage and seeing her reacting to what someone was saying and thinking, 'God, she looks as if she's really concentrating but she doesn't have a line for *ages.*' Whereas I would stand on the stage and look out for friends in the audience and give them little waves till it was time for my line – a habit that did not endear me to directors. So going to rehearsals with Dick got less and less fun as his parts got bigger, and mine got smaller. The crunch came in the summer vacation when we did *A Midsummer Night's Dream* at a hotel outside Stratford. Dick was cast as Demetrius, and I as Hippolyta. Hippolyta has precisely one scene at the beginning of the play and puts in an appearance at the end. And for this we had to live in a caravan in a wet field for six weeks.

Inevitably, we drifted apart, though I always thought of Dick – still think of him – as my first boyfriend, conveniently obliterating Simon. He was certainly my first *love* and I was devastated when, soon afterwards, he started going out with Maria Aitken. But of course there were plenty of other boys for consolation, and in my second year, no longer attached to Dick, I seemed to go out with an awful lot of them. 'Go out with' is a bit of euphemism; I mean I slept with them; I was *wildly* promiscuous. I was still pining for Dick and wanting to find another boyfriend quickly so I thought cut to the chase – rather than waste endless evenings going on dates with men, why not go to bed with them *first* and see if I fancy them?' This was quite an unusual attitude at Oxford at the time and one that gave me a well-earned reputation as an easy lay – I probably slept with about fifty men in my second year. My fantasy in those days was to meet a stranger, exchange almost no words, jump into bed, and then talk afterwards.

But often there was no afterwards, either because the sex was a disaster, or because my pretence of sexual confidence scared them off. I did great, noisy, pretend orgasms with lots of 'Yes! Yes! More! More!' but I still hadn't experienced the real thing. (In retrospect it is really odd that I persisted with sex as long as I did. Normally I'm so terrified of being bored I'll go to the ballet once and say, 'Right, that's it, I tried the ballet and it was boring, won't do *that* again.' But somehow, with sex, I knew it would come right in the end and eventually it did.)

One of the few good men I found in my promiscuous phase was Howard Marks, the Balliol physics student who later became famous as Mr Nice the drugs dealer. He had the same easy attitude to jumping into bed as I did and awarded me the accolade of Great Shag. He stood out at Oxford in those days, not as a jailbird and drugs dealer, but because he was, or claimed to be, a Welsh miner's son who grew up in a pit village where they all spoke Welsh and kept coal in the bath. Later I learned that both his parents were teachers, but he rightly thought that a miner's son sounded more glamorous. He wore blue suede shoes, did brilliant Elvis impressions, and claimed to have lost his virginity to an aunt when he was eight. He was certainly a very experienced and generous lover, probably the first proper Don Juan I ever met, and I was grateful for the sex education he gave me. I never particularly associated him with drugs, though I suppose he smoked pot all the time. But then everyone did. Or actually I didn't, but I pretended I did. I would always take a joint if offered, but I never bought pot myself and didn't miss it in the holidays when I went home to Twickenham. I always preferred cigarettes.

When, if ever, did I do any academic work? I must have done some, to get a second, but I don't remember ever going to lectures. I'm not sure I even knew where they were given, and I certainly never set foot in the Bodleian library. I quite enjoyed studying the history of grammar and etymology; I could write plausible essays on Shakespeare because I'd done him thoroughly at school; I looked for the poets with the shortest canons – the Metaphysicals, Keats, Gerard Manley Hopkins – and avoided those like Tennyson and Spenser who wrote for miles. Ditto novelists – Austen was 'better' than Dickens simply because there was less of her, and I worshipped Fanny Burney because she wrote only one novel. I still haven't read all of Dickens to this day. But I had the advantage of being a quick learner and exams suited me fine – I would bone up the week before, regurgitate it on the day, and then forget it. I totally agree with those who say that coursework is the only proper way to judge academic attainment – while thanking my lucky stars that it didn't exist in my day.

My whole three years at Oxford was a schizophrenic switch between endless parties during term time and then grindingly dull work in the vacations. Not academic work, obviously, but temporary office work. My parents had made me do a secretarial course before I went to Oxford ('something to fall back on') and I had a certificate saying I could do shorthand at 100 wpm and typing at 40 wpm, though I doubt I ever could. But it meant I could sign on with an office temp agency every vacation and work for a few weeks at shipping firms and insurance offices until I had accumulated enough money to pay for my next term's clothes and taxis. Many of the offices were so Dickensian I find it hard to believe they still existed in the 1960s. There were rows of men called 'juniors' in one room and rows of typists called 'girls' (even though many of them were middle-aged) in another, and we would be summoned by successive juniors who would say 'Take a letter, Miss Barber', and start dictating. They spoke so slowly, and so predictably, I never needed to take shorthand – I could have carved the words in granite while they were droning on. The letters were always on the lines of, 'Dear Sir, This to acknowledge receipt of your letter of the 29th ult [ult was just a mystifying way of saying last month]. We are investigating the matters raised in your letter and will vouchsafe our conclusions at a future date.' In other words, piss off. This useless letter would always have to have three copies (which entailed using carbon paper and getting ink all over your fingers), which then had to be put in files and stored in metal cabinets. If you made a mistake in the typing, you would simply start all over again – most offices frowned on Tippex. By the end of the day, my wastepaper bin would always be full of discarded paper and carbon, and on at least three occasions I emptied my ashtray into the bin (of course you could smoke in offices in those days – there was *that*) and started a satisfying bonfire. My normal rate of productivity was about five letters a day – and I was considered an exceptionally efficient worker, highly praised and recommended by my agency. People would work in these offices – the same offices, with the same spider plants – *all their lives* and I believe it was seeing these offices that gave me what little ambition I have. Just as my father was driven by fear of the workhouse that he remembered looming over Bolton in his childhood, I always had this memory of the copy-typing room at the Prudential insurance office, High Holborn, to act as my spur. I panicked as the end of Oxford approached, thinking that I would be swallowed by the Prudential and never seen again. Luckily I met my husband just in time.

David

I met David in the last month of my last term at Oxford and knew immediately that he was The One – the man I must marry. It wasn't just that I fancied him, or wanted to go out with him; I felt I wanted to spend my life with him. I don't know why I was so sure, but I was, and that sureness carried me through more than thirty years of marriage. Even in the bad patches when I thought I might be happier not married at all, I never for one moment thought I could be happier married to someone else. David was the best husband I could ever have or wish for. And I somehow knew that from the moment I met him.

He just appeared in my room one day, with his friend Tim Jeal. I'd met Tim Jeal a few times at parties and maybe he fancied me – at all events it was his idea to bring David to call on me in St Anne's. They had picked up some ticker tape from somewhere and pretended to read it out, they were laughing and shouting, possibly drunk or stoned, and Tim Jeal was talking nineteen to the dozen and running his hands through his sandy blond hair, but I looked at the dark-haired, olive-skinned, blue-eyed man who came with him and thought, He's The One. He made some reference to 'going back to Mexico' in the holidays so I assumed he was Mexican. He had slicked-back hair which looked vaguely Mexican – most undergraduates in those days had Beatles haircuts or long flowing locks. He seemed exotic, mysterious, slightly sinister. I resolved to capture him.

But pursuing him was difficult because we were both frantically revising for finals and moreover he was living in a village outside Oxford, and seldom came into town. It meant I had to spend a lot of time studying bus timetables and hanging round the bus station but, even so, I only managed to bump into him a couple of times. I also met him at a party, and bullied him into taking me to a poetry reading at the Albert Hall, but by the time we left Oxford for good a few weeks later I had made very little progress. I knew he liked me and found me amusing but that was all – he hadn't so much as held my hand.

And then he went off to join his parents in Mexico, and I went back to my parents in Twickenham and worked as a temp typist. I didn't even have his address; I despaired. But one day I ran into an Oxford friend, Nic Mudie, and moaned about the miseries of living in Twickenham and he said, 'Well, actually I've got a house in Stockwell you could live in but it's practically derelict.' He explained that the lease on his mother's house in South Kensington had run out and she'd bought this shell in Stockwell. He was meant to be doing it up but couldn't get a bank loan to start work so it was standing empty. He said casually, 'There's one other person living there – David, that artist bloke from New College – do you know him?' Aaaagh, I sputtered, incapable of speech.

I moved into Groveway, Stockwell, the same day. The house was huge – four floors, at least a dozen big rooms, but many of them uninhabitable with missing window-panes or broken floorboards. The basement and ground floor were crammed, literally floor to ceiling, with furni-ture from the South Kensington house. I had to squeeze between wardrobes and clamber over dining tables even to get from the front door to the staircase. But on the top floor I found three empty rooms more or less intact and a working loo and basin. Moreover, one of the bedrooms had a mattress on the floor and some scattered clothes I thought I recognised as David's. Nic found a mattress for me and a chair. Then he went away and I spent my first night in the house alone, too cold, too terrified, too excited to sleep.

Next day I bought an electric fire and managed to scav-enge another chair, some blankets and a lamp from the furniture piles downstairs. Then I heard the front door open and the slow noisy progress of someone clambering over the furniture and up the stairs. Would it be a burglar or would it be . . . ? 'Oh, hi,' I said, dead casual. 'Nic said I could stay here for a bit. Hope you don't mind.' 'Of course not,' he said. 'I'll help you find some furniture.' So we went and heaved furniture about till lunchtime and ended up with quite a good haul – a very grand bateau-lit bed, two button-back Victorian armchairs and a splendid Tur-key carpet. David said there was a kitchen somewhere in the basement but it was too jammed with furniture to get into, so we went for lunch at a workers' café and then to the Tate Gallery and on the bus back he kissed my cheek, and that was it really.

We spent the whole of that freezing winter in Groveway, and it was one of the coldest winters on record. The first present David ever bought me was a mangy fur coat from Oxfam, which was just what I needed – I wore it to go to the loo. But we managed to make our room into a sort of nest, hung and swagged with every curtain, rug, blanket we could find. We took baths at Camberwell Public Baths, cadged meals off friends, gradually excavated the kitchen and learned to cook – or rather David learned to cook while I signally failed to. He was studying *Larousse Gastronomique* and producing perfect soufflés while I was still struggling with corned-beef hash.

Our friends all said we were 'so brave' to live in Stockwell. Nowadays SW9 is considered a smart address but in those days it was a grim, rundown area, still with lots of bomb damage from the war and horrible rotting council estates. Brixton, a mile up the road, was entirely West Indian; Stockwell was whiter, mainly Irish, but 100 per cent poor. Most of the houses in Groveway were divided into bedsits and all the cars in the road were wrecks that the O'Hagan brothers on the corner were meant to be repairing but never did.

But Stockwell was changing and one day David came back with a strange purple object and said it was an aubergine and he'd bought it in the local greengrocer's. 'Don't you see what this means?' he said, 'It's like the twig the dove brought back to the Ark.' 'No, I don't see,' I said. 'I thought you said it was a vegetable.' So he explained it meant there must be other middle-class people in the area, people who read Elizabeth David, people who knew what to do with an aubergine. It meant the area was 'coming up'. And indeed no sooner had he said it than our street was full of skips and estate agents' signs, and the Irish house over the road that used to have twenty doorbells and a heap of scrap iron in front suddenly had one tasteful brass knocker and a castor-oil plant. Stockwell – and particularly Groveway – was suddenly as hot as Notting Hill is now (Princess Diana would go to dinner parties there a few years later). Which meant that banks were falling over themselves to lend Nic the money to do up our house, and we had to move. It was fine – by then I'd bagged David and would never let him go.

Why was I so sure David was The One? Well, first and foremost, because he was gorgeously handsome and remained gorgeously handsome all his life. People say you shouldn't marry for looks but I disagree: if I tot up all the pleasure I got from looking at David over the years I'd say it amounted to a very substantial hill of beans. Sometimes we'd just be sitting on the sofa watching television and I'd glance sideways at his profile and think, *Gosh!* Also, of course, having a gorgeous husband meant that we had gorgeous children, which I wouldn't have done if I'd married some toad. So his looks were important. But of course there were other qualities too. He had a lovely singing voice and was always singing, everything from Count John McCormack's Irish ballads to music-hall songs. He was a brilliant cook and was never happier than when preparing a fabulous meal. He had a wonderful 'eye' and was always pointing out details – the painting on a pub sign, the brilliant green lichen on a tree stump – that I would not have noticed. I loved going to galleries and museums with him because he taught me so much. He also had the same black sense of humour as me – we both found it hilarious, for instance, that Tommy Cooper dropped dead of a heart attack while performing a television show called *Live from Her Majesty's*. Such bad taste, I know, but it was *our* bad taste and a strong bond precisely because other people disapproved.

Actually we were alike in a million ways – we both hated the theatre, loved opera, hated sport, loved art galleries. We once did a psychometric test for a friend who was training to be a psychiatrist and he said he had never seen two such similar test results. We were both Geminis (though of course we didn't believe in astrology!) and were delighted to be told that Geminis should always marry each other because they made such appalling partners for anyone else – we Twins are the marital lepers of the celestial regions.

On the other hand, we were different in one very important way. David was *good*. He was thoroughly kind, thoroughly truthful, thoroughly decent. Whereas I was somehow morally damaged. I had become a proficient liar in my years with Simon and found it hard to break the habit. I was also apt to do bad things if I thought I could get away with them. But at least I knew I *needed* to marry someone good. I didn't mind having bad hats as boyfriends – in fact I was rather attracted to them – but for a husband I wanted someone 100 per cent decent. Thank God I had the sense to see that.

We came from very different backgrounds. David was not Mexican – that was a misunderstanding – but he grew up mainly abroad because his father worked in different countries as head of the British Council. His father Maurice came from a long line of English gentry – David's middle name, Cloudesley, commemorated one of their ancestors, the admiral Sir Cloudesley Shovel – and had followed his two older brothers to Eton, Oxford and the Guards. He served with distinction as a major in the war and was involved in undercover work in Greece with Paddy Leigh-Fermor (he is mentioned in *Captain Corelli's Mandolin*) and was then appointed head of the British Council in Greece. Later, he was stationed in Italy, Cyprus (where he seems to have played some sort of undercover negotiating role with Makarios), Belgium, Mexico, Thailand and finally Paris. Tall, upright, formal, always immaculately dressed, Maurice was every inch the traditional stiff-upper-lipped English gentleman, but he was not quite as conventional as he appeared. He wrote several rather good travel books and novels under the pseudonym John Lincoln, and he married Leonora, who was an actress and Jewish, i.e. not at all the sort of wife expected in his class. They made a striking couple – he so tall, fair, English, she so petite, dark, Sephardic-looking. David inherited the best of everything – his father's height and china blue eyes, his mother's thick dark hair and olive skin.

As a young boy, David lived with his parents abroad – he remembered idyllic years in Italy and Cyprus – but then, when he was eight, his parents sent him back to prep school in England, and he didn't see them again for over a year. He spent the holidays with his Aunt Anna, Leonora's sister, who was married to a Leeds solicitor and kept a kosher house, so he had to learn the rituals of Judaism at the same time as learning the rituals of boarding school. He hated his prep school so much that he was reluctant ever to talk about it, but he mentioned the cold, the terrible food, the loneliness. Many years later, when our elder daughter Rosie turned eight, David sank into a strange depression and eventually explained it was because he was remembering being sent away to school when he was Rosie's age. Of course it was quite normal then (many expats sent their children 'home' to England at five or six), but whenever Leonora went into one of her raptures about what a doting mother she was, I always had to bite my tongue not to say, 'But you sent David away at *eight*!'

Anyway, he survived prep school, and Eton afterwards, with stoicism but fairly deep unhappiness I think. When, many years later, we used to take a friend's son out from Eton for Sunday lunch, I begged David to at least show me round the chapel, but he never would – he wouldn't even get out of the car. The one saving grace at Eton was that he had a great art teacher, Wilfrid Blunt, who allowed him to stay in the art studio when everyone else was out rowing or playing beastly games. He virtually lived in the art studio and his best friends at Eton were other artists, notably Edmund Fairfax-Lucy, who became an RA, and Nick Gosling, son of the art critic Nigel Gosling, who ran the film society.

David would have liked to have gone to art school but his parents took the conventional line that he must get a proper degree – he could always paint in his spare time.

So he went to New College, Oxford, to read PPP – philosophy, physiology and psychology – a singularly useless degree which, according to David, entirely consisted of observing rats in mazes. More enjoyably, he served on the college art committee and spent many happy days in London choosing prints and paintings for the JCR. He also drew beautiful cover illustrations for *Isis* and other student magazines.

So this was the David I met in 1966. He was far more cultured than me. He had spent more time abroad than he had in England; he had been to the opera at La Scala, and to lunch with Harold Acton at La Pietra; he had visited the Grand Canyon and all the great Mayan temples; he could speak good Italian, French and a little Spanish; he had eaten at Michelin three-star restaurants and could talk about truffles; he knew famous writers and artists like Leonora Carrington, Stephen Spender, Lawrence Durrell, as family friends. On the other hand, I was often surprised by what he *didn't* know. He had hardly been anywhere in England and was thrilled when I later took him to Cornwall and the Lake District. He was terrified of bills, of tax forms, of policemen, of doctors, of any kind of authority. He was also weirdly scared of working-class people – it was always left to me to sort out which cleaner, gardener, plumber, electrician we should hire because he was equally alarmed by them all. Later, when he claimed to have become a Marxist, I said he couldn't really be a Marxist and hate the working class. He said he didn't hate them at all – but he worked on the assumption that they all hated him.

When we first lived together in Stockwell, he was painting and drawing but making no effort to sell his work or even show it to anyone. He had just enough money to live on because his parents were still stationed in Mexico and had put him in charge of letting Little Haseley, their house outside Oxford, and had told him to keep whatever rent was left over when he'd paid the maintenance bills. He filled the house with Oxford friends and we used to go down at weekends to have hot baths and collect the rent.

But when we left Stockwell we needed more money to live on, so David had to get a proper job. An Oxford friend, Paddy Scannell, was helping to set up a brand-new course, media studies, at the Regent Street Polytechnic and said he could get David a few hours a week teaching 'general studies'. David was soon fascinated by the course, and switched from teaching general studies to the history of television, which he thought had been seriously neglected. He and Paddy wrote a book on the early years of the BBC. And, as the course expanded, so did David's responsibilities, until at one point he was head of department. He loved those early years at the Polytechnic, when they were still mapping out the territory of media studies and working to get it accepted as a degree subject.

(I still get furious with people – including, alas, many of my journalist colleagues – who knock media studies as a somehow worthless or frivolous pursuit. I know that the calibre of teaching is not always great, but I don't see how anyone can fault media studies as a *subject*, given that we live in such a media-dominated age. Isn't it important to

71

give young people some idea of how the media works? Can anyone seriously maintain that Latin is more relevant?)

After Stockwell, we had a peripatetic few months, scrounging rooms off friends – one of the advantages of David having been to Eton was that he had plenty of rich friends with spare rooms. We stayed for a while in Oakwood Court, Kensington, one of those grand mansion blocks populated by spies and retired civil servants, and then briefly in Mayfair, in the caretaker's flat in the attic of a beautiful Georgian house. It was a wonderful address and a sweet flat – but unfortunately designed for dwarves. There was only a small patch in the middle of the sitting room where we could stand upright and the double bed was smaller than most children's bunks – we could only make love in the position called 'spoons'. Mayfair, it turned out, was a hopeless place to live. It had no food shops or tobacconists, still less launderettes, and the only place where we could afford to eat was a 'drop-in centre' run by a cult called The Process. We learned to eat very quickly before the sparkly-eyed loonies started asking if we'd found the meaning of life. 'Yep, yep,' we'd say, 'pass the ketchup,' and gulp a few more forkfuls before bolting for the door.

Eventually David ran into a schoolfriend, S, who asked if we wanted to take over his flat in Haverstock Hill, Belsize Park. It was a fabulous bargain – £8 a week for a well-furnished, three-bedroom garden flat overlooking an absolutely glorious half-acre garden. In theory the garden was our responsibility but luckily Mrs Franks upstairs asked if she could sit in it sometimes in return for her tending it. This proved to be an excellent deal because she was a brilliant gardener and responded well to my occa-sional orders – 'More sweet peas', 'No marigolds.' She only put her foot down once when I said we wanted to grow vegetables and she said in her strong German accent, 'This is a nice neighbourhood. I cannot allow.' For once in my life, I had the sense not to argue.

Belsize Park was still in those days a markedly Jewish area with some good delicatessens that closed on Satur-days, opened on Sundays. We lived there for seven years – the only slight mystery was why David's friend S had surrendered this miraculously cheap flat. Eventually Mrs Franks upstairs enlightened us: the man who shared the flat with S had committed suicide one weekend and S came back to find the body. After that, he was unable to live there. Years later, when we left the flat, this had an odd postscript. The landlady asked if we would like to sell her all our carpets, curtains and furniture so that she could let the flat as furnished. We had always assumed that it *was* furnished, by her, but it turned out that all the stuff in the flat belonged to the man who committed suicide. David got in touch with S to ask if he wanted it – he didn't – so David and I acquired this useful legacy of beds and bedding, carpets and armchairs, saucepans and casseroles from a dead man we never met. David would occasionally say, morbidly, 'We're eating off a dead man's plates' and I would say cheerily, 'Yes – aren't they nice!' I still have some of the plates now – it was a strange present from beyond the grave.

We married in 1971, while we were at Haverstock Hill, not because we were particularly hooked on marriage but because in those days you had to be married to get a joint mortgage and we decided we had to buy a house. But we wanted to get married with minimum fuss, in Hampstead Registry Office just over the road. I bought a lovely red Gini Fratini dress, and David wore his best Carnaby Street suit. I said, Do we *have* to ask our parents? And David said yes, we did. So it was wedding with parents at the Registry Office, followed by lunch at the flat and then a party in the evening for all our friends, once our parents had gone. I dreaded our parents meeting – I knew I would squirm with embarrassment – and on the morning of our wedding day I woke up with the most obvious psychosomatic illness of my life: I was literally struck dumb, unable to speak. I managed to croak 'Thank you' when Leonora presented me with a beautiful emerald and diamond ring that had been her grandmother's, and 'I do' in the Registry Office, but when we went back to the flat for lunch with our parents, I spoke not a word. Even when our friends came in the evening, I was still unable to speak, but next day my voice was perfectly normal.

We left Haverstock Hill eventually because it was the Seventies and everyone said you had to get on 'the housing ladder' and buy a house, though we were heartbroken to leave our lovely flat and move from the border of Hampstead Heath to the unknown badlands of Finsbury Park. We arrived at Finsbury Park by the simple process of moving eastwards till we found a house we could afford. Like Stockwell, Finsbury Park was considered way beyond the pale, but we managed to find a very pretty four-bedroom Victorian terraced house with all its original fireplaces and cornices for £14,500 and although, as with Stockwell, everyone said 'You'll be raped and mugged all the time', we weren't even burgled in the ten years we lived there. We were so house-proud, we picked out all the cornices with toothpicks and lovingly sanded and polished the floorboards – the only downside was that huge brown slugs came up through the gaps in the floorboards every night until eventually I insisted on carpets.

I had no decorating taste whatsoever at this stage, but luckily David had more than enough for both of us and, over the years, I learned from him. We made the house really exquisite, though the garden never attained our Haverstock Hill heights. And then, when the house was ready, I stopped taking the pill and waited to get pregnant. David had always been very clear that the whole point of marriage was to start a family – he *longed* to have children. I wasn't sure I did – I seemed to lack any maternal instinct, never played with dolls as a child and never cooed over babies. But David was reassuring: he said if I found I didn't like looking after children, he would do it. I am eternally grateful. If I had married a man who was iffy, who said 'Oh well, you have children if you want to, but on your head be it', I might well be childless today. Thank God David was so sure.

But then I didn't get pregnant for a whole year. It was probably good for me – once I started thinking I couldn't have children then I wanted them badly. And I was haunted by thoughts of the abortion I'd had at Oxford. I'd fallen pregnant almost the first time I slept with an undergraduate, but his brother arranged an abortion at a

75

Harley Street clinic, and I'd had it very quickly and easily and gone to a party the same night. I felt no tremor of guilt or doubt at the time, or for ten years afterwards, but during the months I was failing to get pregnant with David, this blood-spattered baby would come to me in my dreams and say, 'You *could* have had me, you had your chance.' We were actually booked for fertility tests, when we went on holiday to Portugal and bingo!, came back pregnant. Much to my surprise, I loved being pregnant, loved having Rosie, loved breastfeeding, and was very happy to do it all again two years later with Theo. I always wish I'd had more children but we ran out of money and I had to go back to work.

Marrying David was the best, most sensible and 'right' thing I ever did. I believe that to some extent his goodness was catching and that he made me a better person, and certainly a better parent, than I would otherwise have been. I was and still am profoundly selfish, probably as a result of being a spoilt only child, but at least with David around I had some notion of what selflessness looked like. He was very indignant when one of our friends called him a 'saint' – especially as the clear implication was that he was a saint for putting up with me! – and I don't think I would have enjoyed being married to a saint, but I am grateful that I had the sense to marry a good man.

It was an unconventional marriage in some ways. When we first got together in the Sixties, it was extremely unusual for the man to do the cooking, and even our friends often made jokes about it. David's mother was outraged. She was always trying to teach me 'easy' recipes. I resisted.

David loved cooking, I hated it; he was good at it, I was bad. Ergo, why mess up an arrangement that suited us both fine just to fulfil his mother's idea of what wives were supposed to do? Similarly, it was unusual back then for the wife to be the higher earner, as I was for most of our marriage, but it never bothered *us* – it was just a fact of life that journalism paid more than painting or teaching. I think people who try to run their marriages according to other people's expectations are insane. It is quite hard enough to keep a marriage together till death do you part – which I think should be the aim, even if it can't always succeed – without trying to do it to please other people. A good marriage is whatever suits the participants, and our marriage suited us fine.

Penthouse

Marriage first, career second – that was certainly my order of priorities on leaving Oxford, but on the other hand I did need to find *some* sort of employment, and it was by the purest fluke of luck that I stumbled into *Penthouse* magazine. My original plan – to become a film star/billionaire/femme fatale – had not made any progress and when I went to the Oxford careers office the only suggestion they came up with was that I should join the prison service and hope to be fast-tracked into becoming a prison governor one day. What a prospect – especially when I'd put so much hard work into becoming a hedonist! However, it did have the effect of making me think I should apply for some jobs or traineeships, if only to avoid prison.

Like everyone else, I tried for a BBC traineeship but I knew the interview was going badly when they asked what political issues I was interested in, and I scratched my head for a bit and eventually said, 'Er . . . abortion?' – the rejection letter came the next day. I had one secure sellable skill, shorthand-typing, but on the other hand I'd done enough of it to know I didn't want to do any more. The only other thing I knew I could earn money from was journalism, because I'd written a column for the *Richmond and Twickenham Times* while still at school, and kept my hand in at Oxford by writing occasional features for *Isis* and *Cherwell*. But the trouble with journalism in those days was that it was tightly controlled by the NUJ and in order to join any national newspaper you had to go on one of their far-flung training schemes which meant spending two years in the provinces. No way could I do that when I'd just met David, and was in hot pursuit. Anyway, as a lifetime Londoner, Oxford was as far into the sticks as I was ever prepared to go.

So then I started applying to magazines. But they too were largely controlled by unions and also, like the BBC, had this infuriating scam whereby, if you were a woman, they encouraged you to join the organisation as a secretary and 'work your way up'. I didn't fancy two years typing for the editor of *Practical Knitting* while aspiring to the giddy heights of deputy sub-editor. So then I went to see the formidable Beatrix Miller, editor of *Vogue*, who asked what I was interested in. Someone had advised me not to say fashion because that's what everyone said so, bizarrely and quite untruthfully, I said travel (I'd been overland to India in one of my Oxford vacations), and she offered me a job as assistant to the assistant travel editor at £14 a week. I was still mulling this over when I got a better offer from *Penthouse*.

Robert Charles Joseph Edward Sabatini Guccione, a gravel-voiced, Sicilian-American cartoonist and dry-cleaning manager, had launched *Penthouse* in 1965 while I was still at Oxford and caused a great flurry on the high tables by sending out a mailshot to all the senior Oxford dons. Many of them complained about this filth arriving in their pigeonholes so I was despatched by, I think, *Cher-*

well, to interview Guccione and ask why he'd done it. I can't remember anything about our meeting except that it was in a glamorous flat in London and Guccione made me laugh a lot and right at the end he said, 'If you ever want a job, honey, come to me.' I giggled merrily and returned to Oxford but after that I used to say to friends, 'Oh well, I can always go and work for *Penthouse*.'

So, all other avenues having failed, that's what I did. I wrote to Bob Guccione, reminding him of our meeting, and told him I was now a graduate with some experience in journalism and did he have a job on his magazine? I had a letter back from Harry Fieldhouse – Bob didn't really do letters – saying come and see him. Harry was the editor whereas Bob was the 'editor in chief', and he was the one I would be working for.

Everything about *Penthouse* was a surprise. I had imagined that it would be in, well, a penthouse, or at any rate a glamorous West End office, but it was in a tiny terraced house in Ifield Road, off the Fulham Road, looking out on Brompton Cemetery at the back. The front room contained a dolly bird receptionist called Maureen and piles and piles of cardboard boxes – these I was to learn were the tiresome Penteez Panties – with another room housing the Penthouse Book Club at the back. Upstairs, the back bedroom was Bob and Kathy's office, and the front was 'editorial' – a largish room containing the art director Joe Brooks with a very small cubbyhole containing Harry Fieldhouse.

Harry again was a surprise. He seemed very old (I suppose he was about forty) and far too gentlemanly and donnish to be a journalist, let alone editor of *Penthouse*.

1. Possibly my first sighting of Dad

2. On holiday in Lowestoft

3. My mother after she became a beauty

4. David when I first met him at Oxford

5. Studying hard to be a femme fatale

6. My gorgeous kaftan
(*Frances Charteris*)

7. Wedding day, 1971 (*Luke Cardiff*)

8. With Theo (*left*) and Rosie, 1980

9. In sex expert guise
(*Amnon Bar-Tur*)

10. My Penthouse bosses, Bob Guccione and Kathy Keeton
(*AP Photo/Loren Portnow*)

11. The byline photo I used for years (*Ian Cook*)

12. My beloved editor, Harry Fieldhouse

13. Favourite indulgences: me smoking (*Johnnie Shand Kydd*)...

14, 15 and 16. ... and David eating lobsters

17. The mystery picture in the postscript

But there was a dry humour I liked. His first question was, 'Can you spell?'

'Yes,' I said. 'I read English at Oxford.'

'Ecstasy,' he said.

'Well yes, it was very enjoyable.'

'I meant, spell it.'

I resisted the smart-arse answer (i, t) and spelt out e, c, s, t, a, s, y.

'Good. Very few people can spell that word and we use it a lot in *Penthouse*. Pulchritude is another – can you spell it?'

Yes, I said, doing so.

Accommodation, minuscule, predilection, diarrhoea, haemorrhage – he reeled off a list of words and nodded as I spelled them correctly. Then he gave me a short article and told me to underline anything I thought was wrong. There were a few spelling mistakes and I marked them.

'Good,' he said. 'We can pay you £16 a week. The hours are ten to six. Can you start on Monday?'

Yes!

David was waiting for me on the corner and I went running down the street, shouting 'Hooray! Sixteen pounds a week! Starting Monday!' He was as pleased as I was, but asked what the job entailed and of course I had no idea. It didn't matter though. I liked Harry Fieldhouse, I liked the little house in Ifield Road, I knew I would enjoy working for *Penthouse* magazine. And indeed I did, for the next seven years.

On Monday Harry gave me a list of proofreading marks and told me to learn them. My job would be to check all copy that went into the magazine and correct it. The division of labour at *Penthouse* in those early days was very simple: Harry was responsible for all the words in the magazine, Bob for all the pictures; Joe Brooks did the layouts; Kathy Keeton, Bob's girlfriend, was in charge of advertising – but in those days we didn't have any advertising so the magazine was subsidised by its mail-order Penteez Panties and Book Club, run by Maureen and Sylvie downstairs. In theory, the magazine came out monthly; in practice, it came out when Bob had assembled enough money to pay the printers – maybe ten times that first year.

My first weeks on the magazine were leisurely, and I spent many happy mornings arguing with Harry Fieldhouse about the nuances of punctuation and spelling. He had a passionate aversion to 'widows' – odd words at the end of paragraphs that took up a whole line – 'waste of space'. He was very keen on dashes, which I disapproved of in those days (I don't now) and also on *z* spellings – he preferred realize to realise, organize to organise, utilize to utilise. He thought *z* spellings were 'modern' because they were American and he loved anything American which is why (improbably) he adored Bob. He drove a big American car – his Lincoln Townhouse and Bob's Cadillac took up most of Ifield Road. Despite his rather old-fashioned manner, he was an absolute sucker for anything new, innovative – he was what would now be called 'an early adopter'. He was always giving me gadgets that he said would change my life (I could never make them work) and bought himself a sun-tanning bed, imported from America, long before such things were heard of in England. Most disastrously, he had one of the first-ever hair transplants, which resulted in an unfortunate black dotted line across his forehead and a few tufts like lettuce seedlings on his crown. He said they would join up but they never did. I always liked taking strangers into Harry's office and watching their incredulous reaction when they got their first glimpse of his pate.

Bob and Kathy rarely appeared before late afternoon (he suffered from terrible insomnia and if/when he finally got to sleep no one was allowed to wake him), so generally Harry, Joe and I worked quietly in the mornings until Kathy came barking orders in the afternoon. I always loved Bob, for his sardonic wit and gravelly Brooklyn accent, but Kathy Keeton was simply terrifying. She had grown up on a farm in South Africa, trained as a ballet dancer, and become Strip Queen of Bulawayo. In that capacity, she came to London to star at the Pigalle, where Bob spotted her. He found her in her dressing room surrounded by economics books and reading the *Financial Times*. He said he was setting up a magazine and wanted her to model for it – she said no, but she'd come and work for him on the business side. She was earning £150 a week as a stripper. He said he'd pay her £10 a week to sell advertising and she said done. Thus began a partnership as formidable as Antony and Cleopatra, Romeo and Juliet, Dido and Aeneas, Marks and Spencer. He was a good Catholic and stayed married to Muriel, the mother of his four children, until the children were grown up, but Kathy was *maîtresse en titre* and dominatrix of *Penthouse*. She strode around on five-inch stilettos, tossing her mane of tawny hair, her dresses unbuttoned to her waist to show her (somewhat bony) cleavage, barking orders and calling everyone darling, which with her strong South African accent came out as 'dollink'. We called her Miss Whiplash or Princess of Pain – but never to her face because we were all (including Bob, I think) terrified of her.

She couldn't see the point of me at all, but Bob told her I had 'class' – he was impressed by the fact I'd been to Oxford – and she would occasionally stride up to my desk and twirl round, showing off whatever new atrocity she was wearing – a pink vinyl cat-suit maybe, or a leather miniskirt split to the crotch, and ask 'What do you think, dollink?' And I learned to say obediently, 'It's lovely, Kathy.' 'Classy, dollink?' '*Very* classy.' And she would go back to Bob and say, 'It's fine.' She always worried, not without reason, about looking like a hooker.

As I said, the early months were leisurely but our little office soon got busier and busier. The circulation kept increasing, which meant we could afford to pay the printers and publish an issue every month. And the issues got fatter and fatter when Kathy started selling more advertisements. This meant that Harry and I no longer had time for long discussions about semicolons as we were both suddenly worked off our feet. Even Kathy started using me – she made me 'fashion stylist', which meant going round shops begging to borrow bits of clothing – feather boas, cowboy boots, chaps, waspie corsets – for the Pet shoots. Once Kathy came to me and said 'Doll-ink, go to Lillywhites and borrow a black diving suit.' I went to Lillywhites and said I was doing a feature on diving. 'What depth will you be diving to?' they asked. 'Erm – ten miles?' Then, seeing their faces, no, no, I meant ten feet, no, well not very deep – with a harpoon, and a zip down the front. They produced some nightmare orange number. No, no, it has to be black. By this time I had a whole crowd of assistants gawping at me. It was only fear of Kathy that stopped me fleeing from the shop. But finally one of the assistants took pity and said, 'Are we talking a sort of James Bond look?' and produced the zippered black wetsuit I'd been wanting all along. I also had to attend some of the Pet shoots, not with Bob, but with an American photographer called Philip O. Stearns. My duties at the shoots included putting music on the stereo, squirting scent round the room, and powdering the girls' bottoms. In between, I did the *Times* crossword.

Back in the office, I was put in charge of the *Penthouse Forum*, which was Bob's 'classy' title for readers' letters. Friends always assumed I made the letters up but actually I never needed to – the *readers* made them up, densely written twenty-page sagas of how they'd been imprisoned by jack-booted wardresses and subjected to appalling forms of torture and humiliation. My job as *Forum* editor was to try to ensure variety and balance and to prevent the corporal punishment brigade with their endless memories of school beatings taking over the whole section. I was always grateful for a bit of oddity – a foot fetishist now and then, or maybe an aficionado of amputees. But I remember one day I got a letter from Lytham St Annes saying that at the golf club they all put their house keys with an address label in a big pile and you had to draw a key and go to the address and 'pleasure' whatever woman you found there. I said the whole idea was so preposterous we couldn't possibly publish it – it was too obviously made up. Soon afterwards, the *News of the World* ran a great splash on the wife-swapping parties of the Lytham St Annes golf club.

I did some of my first-ever interviews for an interminable series called 'Parameters of Sexuality' about people with odd sexual tastes – a shoe fetishist, countless transvestites and rubber enthusiasts – and I once flew to The Hague to interview a famous old dominatrix who was supposed to lash half the leading politicians in Europe. She was very grand, very funny, and told me that if I ever needed a job she could probably find a role for me in her dungeon. Interviewing these people was a complete doddle because they were always so eager, even grateful, to talk – all I had to do was look interested while they rabbited on. I think I probably developed my interviewing style through those early *Penthouse* confessionals, where the whole trick was not to look embarrassed, not to interrupt or impede their flow, basically just to be a sympathetic ear. I notice that sometimes, even nowadays, when interviewing, say, an Eddie Izzard or a Grayson Perry, I find myself slipping into 'Parameters of Sexuality' mode and asking *only* about their transvestism. Just last year, interviewing Antony Gormley, I got so hooked on asking what it felt like to cover oneself in clingfilm and plaster, and whether he had any related kinks (rubberwear? diving suits?), I temporarily forgot that I was interviewing a famous sculptor.

Another of my jobs was literary editor, which meant buying book extracts and short stories to fill the ever-growing number of pages. The stories had to be 'classy', of course, but they also had to be as long as possible and cost no more than £50. I developed a great hatred of literary agents, who would dump their whole slush piles on me without even the most cursory attention to what *Penthouse* might like – I was bombarded with stories about elderly churchgoing spinsters, which, come to think of it, might have been by Barbara Pym, but they certainly weren't right for *Penthouse*. My great coup, finally, was discovering science fiction and in particular a magazine called *New Worlds* which was publishing J. G. Ballard, Michael Moorcock, Brian Aldiss, Philip K. Dick, but only to a specialist sci-fi audience. They were happy to sell us second British serial rights and we gradually acquired a reputation for publishing good science fiction. In later years Kathy launched a sci-fi magazine called *Omni* in the US, which was hugely successful for a while.

The main requirement for all articles in *Penthouse* was that they had to be long. We ran Q-and-A interviews that rambled on for 30 pages. We had book extracts that were longer than many books. We ran 6,000-word theatre reviews and as much as Kingsley Amis ever wanted to write about booze. The point was that the words pages were printed in black and white and therefore cheap, and the girl pages were printed in colour which in those days was staggeringly expensive, especially as Bob had very high standards. (He worried about colour quality and also about staple lines. It was vital not to put staples through a girl's bosom.) So Harry and I had a very small budget and an enormous acreage of space to fill. We bought book extracts on classical erotica, on alien abductions, on Nazi war crimes. My job was to fillet them, find the juicy bits, and run as long an extract as possible. But always hampered by Harry, who had this obsession with redundancy. He could find extraneous words in any sentence, he could find extraneous sentences in any paragraph, he could find extraneous paragraphs in any page and would merrily run his black fountain pen through them all. But Harry, I would protest, we *need* to make 6,000 words. 'Can't print waffle,' he would say. 'We're writing for *men*!'

(When I started writing for *Penthouse* myself, this became a very personal battle. My ambition was one day to write an article from which Harry would be unable to delete a single word. But there, you see, I've already failed. 'What do you mean *single* word?' he would bark. 'As opposed to what? A hyphenated word?' Even now, long long after he is dead, I still hear that bark in my head. 'Why have you said long long? Is that supposed to mean something different from long? Presumably by your usage, Shakespeare is long long long long long long long long long dead.' As for the word 'very', I still flinch every time I write it. On the other hand, I do sometimes write it now – though I wouldn't have done while Harry was alive – because I believe that readers sometimes need a bit of relaxation in a sentence, as opposed to the rigid terseness – almost telegraphese – that Harry aimed for.)

Of the mail-order ventures that largely subsidised *Pent-*

house when I first joined, Penteez Panties – supposedly erotic gifts for your mistress, actually nylon tat for transvestites, hence the very large sizes – was the more reliable earner, with the Book Society – 'reading matter for gentlemen of discernment' – a close second. The Book Society was housed in the downstairs kitchen, presided over by Australian Sylvie, and attracted our one celebrity visitor – Barry Humphries. His book *Bizarre* was sold through the Book Society and he would drop in occasionally to check sales figures and swop Strine jokes with Sylvie. This was long before he became Dame Edna, but he was already an exotic figure in his big black fedora and cape, and Sylvie would call me downstairs when he came in to share the general hilarity. I remember once whispering to Sylvie 'I think he might be drunk', and I think he might have been. But he was always good fun. Other visitors were less welcome – the country bumpkins who arrived hopefully believing that they would find an office full of Penthouse Pets – *boy*, were they disappointed – or the elderly men who wandered in 'just passing' to say they thought that Miss July might be their long-lost niece and did we happen to have her phone number? Maureen the receptionist would let them ramble on a bit and then say briskly, 'What did you say your niece's name was?' 'Well, Tina,' pointing to the magazine. 'Yeah, well, we never use their real names so she ain't Tina. Bye.' You'd often see men walking along the street and then reeling back in shock when they came to number 170 and thinking they must have the wrong address. We were a very humble little organisation.

But we were expanding. The staff was seven when I joined, but soon we were ten – with a post-room boy, an art assistant, an editorial secretary – and 170 Ifield Road was bulging at the seams. Bob said that he was looking for 'huge new premises' and we all salivated at the thought of moving to a real penthouse in the West End. In fact we moved to an ex-sausage factory in the North End Road, an even less glamorous address than Ifield Road, but here we really did have space and suddenly loads more staff. The magazine by now carried regular advertising and gradually shed its dubious classifieds and reliance on Pen-teez Panties. Bob started an offshoot magazine called *Forum*, which consisted entirely of readers' letters, and briefly (unsuccessfully) launched an upmarket rival to *Gentlemen's Quarterly* called *Viva*.

Actually, *Penthouse* was expanding so fast, it was hard to keep up. I acquired a bigger salary and an office car – a lovely Triumph Herald convertible – and garnered a dazzling array of impressive titles: letters editor, literary editor, arts and reviews editor. It felt like living in a boom and it was fun. Best of all, I acquired a proper expense account in my capacity as literary editor and was greedily developing a major lunch habit. It was the only way, I told Bob, to woo classy writers to the magazine. But then – disaster! – Bob opened the first Penthouse Club in a back alley in Shepherd Market and announced that henceforward all entertaining must be done at the club. This was appalling. No more San Frediano, no more Alvaro, no more Chanterelle. I expected my little flock of writers – Auberon Waugh, Kingsley Amis, Anthony Powell – to rebel, but to my horror they were only too keen to have lunch at the Penthouse Club. Once. Nobody ever wanted to go there a second time. It was a place of Stygian gloom never touched by sunlight. It was rumoured to get lively at midnight, but at lunchtime it always had a sad and listless air, especially when, as often happened, I and my current classy writer were the only customers in the place.

I always arrived early, so I would pass the time chatting to the Pets and hearing about their problems. I remember once, when I was lunching with Auberon Waugh, the Pet came up and did her little bob to Bron as taught – the bob was so that punters could get an eyeful of their cleavage – and then immediately launched into a continuation of our previous conversation: 'My dad got his dialysis machine in the end. He loves it. They put one tube in here and one tube in there . . .' I saw Bron, who had been staring entranced at her cleavage, suddenly turning white as she went into a detailed account of how a kidney machine works. That was often the trouble with Pets – they were meant to be fantasy objects but then they opened their mouths and started chatting about their dad's kidney machine or their mum's emphysema, and somehow the fantasy died. I liked them a lot, the Pets at the club, but I could see that my guests were often sorely disappointed.

In 1969 Bob and Kathy moved to New York to launch *Penthouse* in America, and for over a year we were in the odd position of producing all the copy for the American edition from London because Bob did not yet have an editorial staff there. This meant that, for instance, I was commissioning reviews of Broadway shows and MoMA art exhibitions I would never see from American reviewers I'd never met and hoping blindly that they knew what they were talking about. It also meant that I suddenly had to learn American spelling and (more difficult) American usage – aluminum for aluminium was easy enough, and fender for bumper, gas for petrol, but their use of the word pout (to mean sulk) always caught me out, as did homely, for ill-favoured. I remember, years later, an American editor ringing to ask if I was coming to New York soon and I said no, because I was expecting a baby. She said 'Momentarily?' and I laughed and said, 'Well no, it takes nine months' – I'd forgotten that in America momentarily means soon.

(Another great advantage of this editing-for-America period was that I read an awful lot of American magazines, which stood me in good stead later, when I became an interviewer. My aspirations were always based on the sort of interviews I'd read in *Rolling Stone*, *Esquire*, Andy Warhol's *Interview* and the *New Yorker*, rather than the generally dire standard of interviews in the British press.)

One day Harry called me to his office and said, Have you got your passport? No, of course I hadn't, why would I, in North End Road? So he very kindly drove me home to collect my passport and then to the American embassy to get a visa, and I was on a plane that evening – my first ever trip to the United States. Alas, I was not going to New York but to Milwaukee, via Chicago, to deliver artwork to the printers. Usually Joe Brooks the art director did it, but on his last trip to the States he had been stopped at customs and the customs officers had seen all the *Pent-*

house page proofs in his suitcase and said 'We have a *reader* here' and confiscated the lot. So Bob decided that I would be the best courier in future because no one would suspect me of carrying pornography.

My first few trips were just to Milwaukee, which was boring, but increasingly Bob asked me to come on to New York to collect stuff to take back to London. Often the stuff wasn't ready so I would have to wait several days in New York, which was a great chance to get to know the city. There was only one disadvantage. Bob and Kathy stayed at the Sherry-Netherland and put me up there too, which seemed the height of glamour. But they never gave me any cash. They always said, 'Oh, put it on room service.' But it meant I could never eat anywhere *except* the Sherry-Netherland and I did get thoroughly sick of their menus. With careful budgeting, and use of the subway, I could afford to visit museums and go to and fro on the Staten Island ferry, but then I'd come back and face another evening of room service. I used to spend hours on the phone to David, I was so lonely. Bob occasionally asked if I was enjoying myself and I would say, dutifully, yes thank you. Kathy never asked. Once, when I rang their room and she answered, I said it's Lynn and she sang, very sweetly, 'Happy birthday to you, Happy birthday to you' and said she'd got me a present. Oh, thank you, I said (it was nowhere near my birthday) and asked to talk to Bob. We were mid-conversation when she suddenly snatched the phone back and said, 'You're not Lynn.'

'Yes I am, Lynn Barber from London.'

'Why did you say it was your birthday?'

'I didn't – you did.'

'Don't cheek me, dollink.'

Bob took the phone back to say, emolliently, 'She thought you were her friend Lynn N,' but it confirmed what I'd long suspected, that Kathy didn't even know my name.

Soon afterwards, Bob and Kathy started hiring staff in New York and producing the American edition there, so my services as a courier were no longer required. I was quite relieved, and very untempted when they asked me to come and work for them in New York. By then, I was married to David, buying a house, thinking of starting a family, so it was easy to say no. But I must say English *Penthouse* became very dull once Bob and Kathy moved out. It became almost like a normal magazine, with proper departments, proper deadlines – it was so well-organised it was boring. By the time I left to start a family in 1974 the whole centre of attention had shifted to New York, and London had become a mere branch office.

But I'm glad I worked at *Penthouse* in its chaotic early years. Apart from anything else, it was a wonderful education for me, because we were *so* understaffed I was involved in almost every aspect of the magazine, from ordering stationery to doing layouts to buying book extracts to finding photographic locations. Also, because the magazine was still struggling to survive financially that first year, I developed a fondness for advertisements which you rarely find among print journalists. Most journalists see advertisements as horrid unnecessary intrusions which spoil the look of their pages, but I learned at *Penthouse* to see them as lifesavers that would pay my salary for the next three months. When Kathy strode through the office shrieking 'I've got Lufthansa!' or 'Six months of Dormeuil!' we would crack open the (Spanish) champagne and celebrate her success. The fact that Harry then lost us the Lufthansa ad by putting it in the middle of an article about Nazi war atrocities was, I remember, the first time I ever doubted his sagacity. He said it wasn't his job to know which ads went where but I thought it should have been.

People assume that the *Penthouse* office must have been a hotbed of sex but it certainly wasn't when I was there. Of course there were odd trysts in the stationery cupboard but no more than you would get in any office. Both Bob and Joe Brooks were businesslike when it came to choosing Pets – I remember Bob once saying, 'We're so successful now I don't have to seduce the girls to get them to pose.' Joe the same: the choice of Pets was far too serious to waste on the casting couch. Maybe there were abuses lower down the hierarchy – I've heard of freelance photographers telling girls 'Be nice to me and I'll get you into *Penthouse*' – but there are slimy freelancers in every branch of journalism.

In later years, when I became respectable, I would have to defend myself from feminist attacks – How *could* you work for a soft-porn magazine? Very easily, as it happened. I've never had a problem with pornography. I think schoolboys and lonely old men need something to wank over and *Penthouse* was more tasteful than most wank mags. As for whether the Pets were exploited – I don't think they were. They were well paid and we took care to protect their identities if they requested it. We had a swap system with *Lui* in France, and I think a Swedish magazine as well, so that if we found a girl who didn't want to have her pictures published in England because her parents might see, we would exchange her with a French or Swedish girl who had similar reservations. Bob was always keen to find 'virgins' – not literally, but girls who had not done glamour modelling before. Of course they often lied and said they hadn't when they had, but this was the late 1960s, early 1970s, and quite a lot of girls were willing to strip off. If they were voted Pet of the Year, they were launched on a career, much like a Miss Britain or Miss World, and several of them went on to greater things.

But to get back to the question: was I ashamed to work for *Penthouse*? No – on the contrary, I am proud of it. I know it probably seems deluded now, but we really *did* feel that we were part of the sexual revolution, fighting a crusade against censorship. When I joined *Penthouse* there wasn't even a proper vocabulary for talking about sex; half the nitty-gritty was still in Latin – fellatio, cunnilingus, even 'membrum virile'. We cheered when the Lord Chamberlain abandoned theatre censorship; we positively thrilled when underground magazines like *It* and *Suck* came out – I still remember the latter's great front page 'Twenty Famous Fannies and How They Taste', starting with Golda Meir. I did witness, by being there, the whole sexual revolution and the death of censorship. Of course everyone now argues that it's all gone too far but I remember the dark ages before the sexual revolution, when the *fear* around sex was astonishing. The only sex education we got at school was a lecture on menstruation, a lecture on reproduction in the frog and then – bewilderingly – a lecture on venereal disease. They are so entwined my memory that I still can't see a frog without wondering if it is suffering from tertiary syphilis. So anything that helped demystify the subject, that gave people the vocabulary to talk about it, could only be a good thing – and I would include *Penthouse* in that.

Actually I played my own little part in the sexual revolution by briefly becoming a sex expert. It started in 1973, when things were getting boring at *Penthouse* so I was bashing out freelance articles for the women's magazines under a variety of different bylines – 'Should I sleep with him before marriage?', 'How can I tell if he's faithful?' Then I wrote one called 'How to improve your man in bed', which provoked a huge response. So when, a few weeks later, a *Penthouse* photographer called Amnon Bar-Tur announced that he was setting up a publishing house and did I have a book in me, I said yes, it would be called *How to Improve Your Man in Bed*. Amnon barely spoke English but he knew a great title when he heard it, and signed me on the spot, for £500. I thought that was a lot of money – it didn't even occur to me to ask for royalties.

I wrote the book in two months and it sold around the world. It was a novelty at the time because sex manuals written by women were almost unknown – the only one I can think of is Marie Stopes's *Married Love*, which was published in 1918. Actually there were very few helpful sex manuals of any sort. Until *The Joy of Sex*, the field was dominated by a writer called Robert Chartham who wrote endless books called *Sex Manners for Men*, *Sex Manners for Women*, *Sex Manners for Couples* etc, which were all weirdly obsessed with undressing rather than sex. They had pages and pages on how to remove a woman's bra without her noticing – a pretty futile activity, I would have thought – but it was typical of what in those days was called 'the art of seduction'. They were books for chaps who basically wanted to manoeuvre a woman into bed without her having a chance to object – not quite date rape but getting on that way.

I was tackling a more realistic problem: how to make your boyfriend a better lover without actually *telling* him what to do. It seems incredible in retrospect, but in those days you really couldn't say to a man, 'This is my clitoris, *here*', because many men had no idea what a clitoris was or what to do with it, and giving instructions would have been considered outrageously bossy. So my advice was to proceed as for ballroom dancing when you are partnered by some idiot with two left feet and have to somehow steer him in the right direction without appearing to lead. The whole book seems impossibly quaint now, but it was well-intentioned and quite useful for its time.

Amnon, being a photographer rather than a publisher, simply sold the manuscript on to a real publisher called Heinrich Hanau (later prosecuted for publishing *Inside Linda Lovelace*) and concentrated on taking my photo for the book jacket. This involved weeks of squabbling, with Amnon producing garments he considered sexy and me rejecting them. In the end I consented to wear a long silver dress and five-inch heels and recline on a chaise longue in a sophisticated manner. I also gave interviews, appeared on *Call My Bluff*, and wrote endless spin-off articles for the women's magazines. Poor David had to put up with his Polytechnic students asking him 'Are you improved?', but he took it all with good grace. The only really nasty moment was when the *News of the World* sent a reporter to doorstep my mother at the school where she was deputy head, to ask what she thought of my book. She was able to answer truthfully that she hadn't read it and didn't intend to.

The book sold well in England but, more importantly, went on to sell around the world. *Mehr Spass Mit Mannern*, *Maak je man meer mans in bed*, *Como Mejorar al Hombre en la Cama* (the Spanish edition, which had a particularly hilarious cover of a man looking suicidal while being nuzzled by a blonde). Years, *decades*, later I would suddenly get letters requesting Portuguese rights, or Hungarian – you could almost track the progress of sexual liberation around the world by the date each country started publishing *How to Improve Your Man in Bed*. And for many years afterwards, passing through foreign airports, my eye would suddenly be caught by my own name in a bookshop and I'd think, 'Oh, I've reached Brazil, have I?' with a little glow of pride.

Unfortunately I'd sold all the rights to Amnon so I made no money from my international bestsellerdom. But because *How to Improve* was such a success, I had a huge offer from Simon & Schuster in the States to publish a follow-up and this time, thank God, had the sense to get an agent. The follow-up was meant to be called *How to*

Play Around Happily but then the publishers got cold feet and called it *The Single Woman's Sex Book* – an inferior title but then it was a vastly inferior book. The trouble was I'd said everything I wanted to say about sex in *How to Improve Your Man in Bed*, and really had nothing to add. Moreover, I was breastfeeding Rosie when I wrote it, and found it really hard to enthuse about foreplay while worrying about cracked nipples. So my career as a sex expert effectively began with my first sex book and ended with my second. But at least it tided us over financially and enabled me to give up work and start a family.

There was an odd postscript to my *Penthouse* years. In 1983, when I was still fairly new on the *Sunday Express* magazine, the editor Ron Hall decided to do a series on 'the new millionaires' – new in the sense that they were not besuited City types – and suggested that I should interview Bob Guccione. So I wrote to him in New York and got an instant yes. Bob was then probably at the height of his success. *Penthouse* was regularly selling over three million a month (and would achieve five million when it had Miss America on the cover in 1984) and had overtaken *Playboy* in news-stand sales. Moreover the sci-fi magazine *Omni*, which Kathy launched in 1979, was doing well, especially in Japan, though it never attained its one-million circulation target. In 1982 *Forbes Magazine* put Bob's net worth at $400 million. He had bought a mansion on the Upper East Side that was supposed to be the largest private house in Manhattan, and he had begun to amass his 'museum-quality' collection of Impressionist and Modern artworks. He had come good even perhaps beyond his wildest dreams and Kathy was still by his side.

I wanted to laugh when I saw the house – it was the purest *Citizen Kane*. You walked down a long marble hall with a 'Roman-style' swimming pool with pillars and mosaics to your right, till you came to a reception area covered with gloomy Old Masters – a Pietà, a Deposition from the Cross – and a wall of sixteenth-century linen-fold panelling that swung away at the touch of a button to reveal a cinema screen. Downstairs in the basement was the gym and a catering kitchen and a security bunker with battalions of security goons watching CCTV screens. The whole house was infested with giant dogs, Rhodesian Ridgebacks, which belonged to Kathy. She gave me a guided tour later, pointing out her '24-carat gold mosaic step-in whirlpool tub' and all the loos and washbasins 'carved out of one solid block of finest Italian Carrara marble'. She looked *exactly* the same as I remembered her and still called me 'dollink'.

Bob was wearing his usual absurd clothes – powder-blue suede trousers, silk baseball jacket unzipped to reveal his tons of medallions – but he'd had his hair woven or something. Also – amazingly – he had stopped smoking and even been on holiday for the first time in his life, and started to sleep normal hours. He seemed relaxed, happy, and very keen to show me his art collection – a lovely Degas of a girl drying herself after a bath, a pink-period Picasso, a Matisse, Rouault, Chagall, Vlaminck, Renoir. When he was a boy, he said, he had a book on French Impressionist art and whenever he saw one of the paintings illustrated in that book for sale, he tried to buy it. He was hurt when I asked if they were genuine, and showed me all the auction catalogues with the prices scribbled in, and told me I could speak to his dealer – he had someone out bidding for a Rouault at that moment.

But then he started talking about his other projects – building a casino-hotel complex in Atlantic City in order to fund his atomic fusion plant. His what? Apparently he had a team of scientists in San Diego working to design an atomic fusion plant that, if successful, would revolutionise the energy industry overnight. But he needed to fund it with the income from his Atlantic City casino which wasn't yet built. It was held up for years by an FBI investigation into his supposed Mafia connections – they eventually cleared him of any involvement and granted a gaming licence, but meanwhile the half-built casino had already gobbled up $74 million of his own money. I thought the scheme sounded mad at the time, but on the other hand Bob's schemes always sounded mad – perhaps it would work. But in the event it was these *grands projets* that were to be his downfall.

The interview is etched in my memory not only because it was the last time I saw Bob and Kathy, but also because it was the first time I 'found myself' as a writer and started developing my own style. The visit was also memorable because Joe Brooks, the art editor from London who'd moved to New York with Bob and Kathy, took me out to lunch and at the end ran his hand down my cheek and said 'Do you want to have sex?' 'No thank you, Joe,' I said politely. 'Sure? OLDC?' [On location doesn't count – a

102

well-worn line in film and media circles.] 'Yes, absolutely sure, thank you, though it's very kind of you to ask.' I was not being ironic. Joe Brooks was a famously expert lover, the Warren Beatty of the magazine world, whereas I was a rather frayed Finsbury Park mother, whose figure even at its best had never come up to *Penthouse* standards. So it *was* kind of him to ask. But I also found it easy to say no.

When the article appeared I sent a copy to Bob Guccione and Joe Brooks rang and said, 'He says he'll kill you if you ever set foot in New York. He didn't like what you said about Kathy.' I took this threat sufficiently seriously to feel a little tremor of anxiety on all my subsequent trips to New York, and when Graydon Carter of *Vanity Fair* tried to persuade me to move there in the mid-1990s, a fear of running into Bob and Kathy was one (albeit a very minor one) of many considerations that convinced me to say no.

But of course I've followed the *Penthouse* story at second hand, from the press and from gossip from other *Penthouse* ex-employees. Having worked for *Penthouse* is rather like having been to an obscure but colourful prep school subsequently closed by scandal – once you meet someone with whom you have this past in common you can talk of nothing else. Thus I learned that Bob finally married Kathy in 1988, and that she had a boob job around then (someone told me that she looked 'like a skeleton with a lilo strapped to her chest'). She was diagnosed with breast cancer in 1995 and given only six weeks to live, but she fought it off with a controversial new drug and finally died, during surgery, in 1997. By then the

Penthouse empire was crumbling – partly because the magazine was undercut by internet porn but also because Bob lost about $100 million in his failed attempts to build the Atlantic City casino and the nuclear cold fusion plant (at one point he was supporting eighty-two scientists in San Diego) and because in 1992 he had to borrow $80 million to pay his tax bill. Sadly, he had also fallen out with his sons Bob Jnr and Tony and refused to see them, even when he was diagnosed with throat cancer. Bob also made the bad decision to take *Penthouse* downmarket in response to internet porn – by the late 1990s it was showing penetration and even 'water sports'.

In a desperate last play to appease his creditors, Bob sold his art collection in Sotheby's in 2002 but, whereas it had been valued at $59 million just two years earlier, it fetched only $19 million. It wasn't enough: the *Penthouse* empire was declared bankrupt in 2003, and Bob was evicted from his mansion the next year. By this time he had advanced throat cancer and was being fed by a tube to his stomach. He looked awful in the last photos I saw. I'm not sure where he lives or what he does now. I remember him with affection and deep gratitude for giving me my entrée to journalism.

Fleet Street

Our first daughter, Rosie, was born in 1975 and our second, Theo, in 1978, and I didn't go back to work till 1981 so I served my stretch as a stay-at-home mother. I did it with reasonably good grace, I hope, though I still go cold at the words 'playgroup duty' or, worse still, 'papier mâché'. Luckily Finsbury Park at that time was absolutely seething with saintly mothers who would ring and say they planned to spend the afternoon making papier mâché masks and would my daughters like to join in? Would they just! The problem came when I had to offer some equivalent treat. Luckily I soon discovered that the biggest treat you could give these middle-class Finsbury Park children was to plonk them in front of the telly, because they weren't allowed to watch telly at home. There was as much puritanism around television in those days (the early Eighties) as there is around, say, recycling or food additives now. But David could say, and often did say, with the authority born of his media-studies research, that it was positively *good* for children to watch television. The consequence was that our daughters, who were allowed to watch as much television as they liked, rarely bothered to, while their friends sat glued to our box.

The only writing I did during these playgroup years was a hefty tome called *The Heyday of Natural History* about the effect of Darwinism on popular Victorian natural history books. It seems completely mad in retrospect but my thinking was that it would be easier, with children, to write an historical book based on library research than to flit around doing freelance journalism. Boy, was I wrong! The book got excellent reviews, and still counts as my calling card with people like Sir David Attenborough, but I bitterly regret doing it. It was five years' hard work, for almost no money, and proved what any of my Oxford tutors could have told me – that I had no natural vocation for scholarship. The saddest outcome was that, before I wrote *Heyday*, I used to love reading Victorian natural history books and searching for them in second-hand bookshops, but afterwards I could hardly bear to look at them, even the real beauties like Philip Gosse's *Tenby*.

It was dear old Harry Fieldhouse who got me back into journalism. He had left *Penthouse* and I'd lost track of him. But apparently he was working at the *Telegraph* Magazine and told the editor that I was an expert on natural history (ha!) and therefore the right person to interview the Nobel Prize-winning ethologist Konrad Lorenz in Vienna. The commission came completely out of the blue (I didn't know then that Harry was behind it); I hadn't done any journalism for years and in fact had never interviewed a heavyweight scientist like Lorenz, but of course I was thrilled to go to Vienna. I worried beforehand that Lorenz would be too dry a subject, but he proved to be an extraordinarily charming, cultured, fascinating man, and I remember lying in my Viennese hotel room thinking, 'This is amazing – I am being *paid* to meet someone I would kill to meet anyway.' Until then, I hadn't had any particular ambition, but suddenly at thirty-six I knew what I wanted to do – interviewing, and lots more of it.

Soon afterwards, Harry Fieldhouse got in touch and said he was working for the new *Sunday Express* colour supplement and would I like to join? Would I? I was *dying* to get back to work after six years of Finsbury Park domesticity and by now we were desperate for money. Also it meant that I would at last be working in Fleet Street, though I didn't realise then that I would be witnessing its dying days. I loved watching the flatbed trucks bringing great rolls of newsprint from Scandinavia, and unloading them down chutes into the bowels of the Express building, aka the Black Lubyanka. I loved the feeling of being part of an industry, of having some connection with the lumberjacks who felled the trees, the paper millers who turned them into newsprint, the lorry drivers who drove them across the Continent, the printers who – sometimes, when they weren't on strike – printed the pages. The back stairs of the Black Lubyanka were thickly coated with ink from the printers' hands and you could hear, and even feel, the great shuddering roar in the late afternoon when the presses started to roll.

And of course I loved going through the famous art deco lobby to collect my expenses in 'the bank in the sky'. Such fabulous expenses too! The first time I ever filled out an expenses form, the deputy editor told me it was 'pathetic'. What did I mean travelling second class on the train or, worse still, by tube – didn't I know that NUJ regulations meant we were only allowed first-class train travel and taxis? And those terrible cheap restaurants I frequented! It was against all his principles to approve a lunch bill for only £6. He passed me a stack of blank restaurant receipts and told me to try harder next time. In those days, it was completely normal for journalists to ask for half a dozen receipts every time they paid a restaurant bill. And if you were going on a trip abroad, you went up to the bank in the sky for an advance of £300 or £500 with no explanation at all.

Altogether, the *Sunday Express* was by miles the most fun of anywhere I've ever worked and I made some very good friends there. We'd roll up about ten-thirty or eleven, open our mail, discuss what we'd done the night before, read the newspapers (for some reason we *all* had to read *all* the papers every day), but the really important business of the morning was making arrangements for lunch. If one of us was 'entertaining a contact' we'd go to a grand restaurant like the Savoy Grill or Rules; otherwise we'd go to the nearby Italian, Capitelli's, or to Joe Allen in Covent Garden, or to the unbelievably seedy City Golf Club where the food was terrible but you got the very best and latest Fleet Street gossip. There were three-bottle, four-bottle, six-bottle lunches and it was a poor lunch indeed that finished before four o'clock. Occasionally, we'd all have to 'help' our wine writer, Oz Clarke, with a wine tasting, which meant the office would be awash with bottles for days. I was supposed to take notes of Oz's comments but after the first few bottles I could never read my own handwriting. Insofar as I did any work, I tended to do it at home before I left for the office.

My first job at the *Sunday Express* was writing the weekly 'back of the book' celebrity interview called 'Things I Wish I'd Known at 18'. It was one of those one-page single-quote formats, like the *Sunday Times*'s 'Life in the Day of', where you cobbled all the quotes together to make a continuous narrative. I wasn't crazy about the format or the subject – everyone said they wished they'd learned more languages and kept up the piano – but I found that just asking people what they were like at eighteen, on the cusp of adulthood, was often quite revealing. And it was good practice in dealing with celebrities, so that I got over the usual beginner's problem of being star-struck. Of course I was always 'thrilled' to meet them, but not so thrilled that I forgot to ask questions. But the really good discipline was learning how to vary the pieces every week when the format was so tight. It taught me always to listen for the differences between people rather than the similarities, and to cherish their idiosyncrasies of speech.

I had a memorably enjoyable interview with Sir Ralph Richardson, though he was most peculiar on the phone beforehand. (Incidentally, in those days, you could often find famous people's phone numbers in *Who's Who* or even in the London phone book. You didn't have to go through a million PRs as you do today.) Sir Ralph readily agreed to do the interview but then said, 'And what will you pay me?' I said, shocked, 'Oh no, we don't pay for interviews.' He said, 'Don't *you* get paid, my dear?' I said, oh yes, *I* did. 'But I thought you said it was all in my own words?' Er . . . yes. I was beginning, rather belatedly, to see the difficulty. 'Tell you what,' he continued, 'I'll write it myself and then you can pay me. But I don't want a cheque, I want a case of wine from Berry Bros. and Rudd. Tell them it's for me – they know what I like. Now when do you want to come and interview me?' I put the phone down deeply puzzled, but when I told my editor he just laughed and said oh yes, and presumably sent the wine because Sir Ralph welcomed me warmly when I arrived. He talked so seamlessly and entertainingly, he easily earned his case of wine.

The most embarrassing interview I ever did was with Robert Robinson, who was ubiquitous as a radio and tele-vision quiz-master at the time. I took a taxi to his smart house in Chelsea and – as often in those days – I had chew-ing gum in my mouth and dumped it in the taxi ashtray when I got out. Mrs Robinson let me in, introduced me to her husband, but we were still standing in the hall when the doorbell rang. Robert Robinson opened the door, and an irate taxi driver slammed my lump of chewing gum into his hand, screaming 'Filthy habit!' The man turned on his heel to go, but then he did a double-take and spun back again – he had suddenly recognised Robert Robinson from the telly. His manner changed instantaneously from pit bull to poodle. 'So sorry, sir,' he whined. 'If I'd known it was you ...' Then, fatally, he tried to retrieve the chewing gum from Robinson's palm, but the gum was stuck and the more the cabbie tried to grab it, the more it stretched between their two hands, until finally, stretched to breaking point, it sank in coils on the exquisite carpet. Mrs Robinson gave a little wail and looked as if she might cry. I stood dumbstruck, too embarrassed even to apologise. The interview never really recovered.

I also had a weirdly embarrassing encounter with Alan Whicker. He lived on Jersey and kindly invited me to lunch at his house. He was a bit stiff, I thought, but perfectly courteous and we proceeded through lunch. He was talking about being eighteen during the war, and how strange it was, boys pretending to be men, far away from home, and how quickly all your values changed. I asked – because it seemed apropos – whether he'd ever been to prostitutes, and without saying a word, he slammed his napkin down on the table and stalked out of the room. I sat there for about five minutes wondering what to do. Then he stalked back in again, holding a piece of paper, and read from it, like a barrister reading from a brief: 'I put it to you, Miss Barber, that you used to work for *Penthouse* magazine and are the author of a book entitled *How to Improve Your Man in Bed*.' 'That's right,' I said amiably, wondering what was coming next. Did he want a signed copy or something? We both stared at each other, baffled. Then he went out again, came back, picked up his napkin and resumed the meal. I think, in retrospect, he thought this was the great moment of truth when he dragged the skeleton out of my closet and exposed me as the shameful pornographer I was. But in fact my skeleton had never been closeted – everyone who knew me knew I worked for *Penthouse* and wrote sex books. But I didn't feel I could repeat the question about whether he ever went to prostitutes!

(Incidentally, asking men whether they've ever been to prostitutes – or, similarly, whether they've ever had a homosexual encounter – is one of those Russian roulette questions where you have no idea beforehand what reaction you will get. I always work on the basis that people shouldn't be offended by a *question* – after all, they only have to say 'No, never' – but unfortunately some people, obviously including Whicker, seem to regard a question as tantamount to an accusation. I still think it's worth asking, though, because the reaction itself is informative.)

After I'd been working at the *Sunday Express* magazine for about a year, under Charles Wintour, we were told we were getting a new editor – Ron 'Badger' Hall, who had just been sacked from the *Sunday Times* magazine. (*Private Eye* had christened him Badger because he walked like a badger, with inturned toes.) Now as it happened I knew Ron Hall from way, way back, because he'd been a friend of Simon's friend Danny and I'd met him sometimes at Bedford Square. He'd also propositioned me once or twice, but I hoped he'd forgotten that. In fact I hoped he'd forgotten he'd ever met me. But apparently he hadn't because almost on his first day at the *Sunday Express* he whisked me off to lunch at the Zanzibar and said, 'I know you're wonderfully indiscreet – give me the lowdown on all your colleagues' – which of course I merrily did.

He said he thought I could write longer articles than just the 'Things I Wish' format and he said the first one he wanted me to do was a cover story on Auchtermuchty. Huh? What is Auchtermuchty? 'Don't you read John Junor's column?' he snapped. John Junor was the editor of the *Sunday Express* and wrote a column in which, I learned, he frequently referred to Auchtermuchty. It was a small town he passed through on his way to the Royal and Ancient Golf Club at St Andrew's but for some mysterious reason he had appointed it his personal Brigadoon, and often wrote tongue-in-cheek panegyrics to the Elders of the Kirk of Auchtermuchty.

My article, it turned out, was intended as a diplomatic olive branch. Up till now, Junor had never spoken to anyone on the magazine. The Express management had insisted that the *Sunday Express* must *have* a magazine, to compete with its rivals, but Junor flatly refused to acknowledge its existence. Ron Hall was hoping that if I wrote a lavish encomium to Auchtermuchty, John Junor would be so flattered that good relations would ensue. In particular, Ron insisted, I must persuade the Elders of the Kirk of Auchtermuchty to pose for a group photograph. He would then have it blown up and framed and would present it to Junor as a token of their new friendship, much like Chairman Mao's gift of giant pandas to President Nixon in 1972.

I'm not sure I realised what an enormous diplomatic responsibility was resting on my shoulders. All I knew was that I had to write a great long article about an obscure Scottish town. Ron said it would be easy: I would park myself in the pub and chat to the inhabitants and interesting stories would inevitably emerge. That, he said, was how *real journalists* operated. Well, ha bloody ha. I got to Auchtermuchty and went into the pub at lunchtime and everyone reeled back in horror, never having seen a woman in the pub before. And when I say 'everyone' I mean the half-dozen decrepit alcoholics who constituted its entire clientele. I was branded the Scarlet Woman within ten minutes of my arrival in Auchtermuchty and word travelled fast in that uptight little town. When, later that afternoon, I went to the school gate thinking I could chat to mothers collecting their children, they ostentatiously turned their backs on me – they knew I was that English hussy who'd been seen entering the pub.

By the end of the day I had spoken to precisely no one and rang Ron in despair, quoting one of his own favourite lines, 'If at first you don't succeed, give up.' Normally he would have laughed, but he was terrifyingly firm. 'You have *got* to write this article, Lynn, and you must stay in Auchtermuchty as long as it takes. There is no job for you here without it.' I almost abandoned my career in journalism on the spot. But gradually over the days – it felt like years – I managed to strike up conversations here and there and finally assembled the Elders of the Kirk of Auchtermuchty for their group photo. It did the trick. John Junor was flattered, Ron Hall was delighted, my job was safe. But that week in Auchtermuchty was the longest, hardest, most gruelling assignment of my life, and when, in later years, I sometimes fell among foreign correspondents reminiscing about all the wars and horrors they had seen, I would add my plaintive twopennyworth: 'I never went to Afghanistan, Iraq or Kosovo, but I did once spend a week in Auchtermuchty . . .'

After my Auchtermuchty triumph, I was given bigger and better stories to write, and all was going swimmingly till I suffered a slipped disc that put me in hospital for months and left me permanently lame. The last interview I did before going into hospital was with the Sixties pop singer Sandie Shaw, over lunch at the Neal Street restaurant in Covent Garden. She arrived an hour late, with a boyfriend whose name she never divulged, and everything about her infuriated me. She said she didn't really do lunch, and started ordering off-menu, a leaf of this and a dab of that. She answered all my questions with sulky yes/no answers or snorts of boredom. By this time I was in a lot of pain from my slipped disc and I suddenly exploded, 'I've had enough of this. I don't want to be here any more than you do. I'm going into hospital for an operation tomorrow and I don't give a toss about your poxy little career. Just eat your lettuce leaf and go home.' She immediately transformed into a quite different person. Oozing sympathy and concern, she asked about my operation and said forcefully, 'You must not let them operate on your spine. It is what connects your brain to the Earth. I will chant for you. I will get my group to chant for you. Here is the chant you must learn.' Then, in the middle of the Neal Street restaurant, she went into a long na-na-gong routine (apparently her chant was the same as Lynne Franks's, i.e. Edina's in *Ab Fab*), deftly snatched the bill, paid it, and put me in a taxi home. Somehow she also got my phone number because she rang David a few days later when I was in hospital and told him she was chanting for me every day. She tried to teach him the chant but he said it didn't accord with his faith (atheism, like mine, but he didn't tell her that) and she said of course she respected different beliefs. Anyway, she proved to be very kind when it mat-

115

tered, though a bit too mad for my taste.

My long stay in hospital had a markedly stiffening effect on my character. I emerged with far more courage than I'd had before, more willingness to say no, less eagerness to please. And soon afterwards I did the interview with Bob and Kathy in New York that proved to be a great turning point in my career. Up till then, I'd always written interviews in the third person, which was the convention then. Even if you had to mention yourself for some reason it was always in the guise of 'your reporter' or 'the present writer', because it was felt that journalists must serve the great god objectivity and never intrude into their own articles. I'd gone along with the convention quite obediently – I still thought of myself as a novice – but when it came to writing about Bob and Kathy I felt I *had* to say that I'd worked for them for seven years, and that it would be dishonest not to.

I explained all this to Ron Hall but, as an old *Sunday Times* hand, he was deeply wedded to the objectivity convention and said it was 'unprofessional' and 'girlie' to write in the first person. But, with my new hospital courage, I dug my heels in and said I couldn't write it any other way. Eventually he conceded: 'Well try writing it your way but then, if I say it doesn't work, you must write it my way.' I agreed. I wrote it my way and he never mentioned his way again. From then on I wrote all my interviews in the first person and felt I'd finally found my voice. I never believed in 'objective' interviews anyway – if there are two people in the room, you can't pretend the interviewee is talking into space. I wrote with increasing confidence

116

and soon afterwards, in 1986, won my first British press award.

The next year I won the award again for the only 'world exclusive' scoop of my career – an interview with John Paul Getty II. Getty in those days was a recluse who had fled from Rome in 1972 after his wife Talitha Pol died of a drugs overdose, and had been holed up for years in Cheyne Walk. But there had been recent rumours that he was staying in the London Clinic suffering from an obscure circulatory problem. So when my colleague Pauline Peters said she needed help with a phone-round asking foreigners why they chose to live in England, I decided to ring Getty at the London Clinic. I was put through immediately, and he chatted away about his love of England and particularly cricket. I typed up the quotes and gave them to Pauline, whereupon everyone in the office fell about and said it was a well-known fact that Getty never gave interviews and I must have been speaking to an impostor. 'But that's ridiculous,' I said. 'I'll phone him again.' So I rang the London Clinic, asked to be put through to Mr Getty, and the receptionist said, 'Oh no, he never takes calls.'

So then it became a sort of crusade for me to get an interview with John Paul Getty just to prove that it *was* him I'd spoken to on the phone. I kept writing to him every week, never getting an answer. But then I wrote to his solicitor, Vanni Treves, and Vanni Treves invited me to his office and said Mr Getty never gave interviews, but he might agree to meet me for a chat provided I didn't have a notebook or tape recorder or anything to remind him I was a journalist. (He hated journalists from the time his son had been kidnapped in Rome and he had been hounded by the press.) Treves said, 'I'll call you when the time is right.' So that's what happened: he called me one afternoon, said 'Come over to St James's Place', met me on the street and took me up to Mr Getty's apartment. Mr Getty didn't exactly *chat* – he was watching golf on television – but he let me look around the apartment and admire his beautiful old wind-up gramophone and Gustave Moreau paintings, and he answered enough of my questions to make a decent article. It was a world exclusive when it was published because it was the first interview with Getty – almost the first sighting of him – for well over a decade. In later years, he became much more sociable and quite often invited journalists to attend the cricket matches at Womersley, his country estate, so my scoop evaporated (as scoops tend to do), but it was enough to win me another press award.

As the *Sunday Express*'s only 'award-winning writer', I was well looked after at the paper, with a generous salary, lavish expenses, a company car, my pick of travel freebies and a beautiful office (when we moved over Blackfriars Bridge) overlooking the River Thames. I had virtually all the perks a journalist could hope for – except recognition. It was depressing that nobody I knew ever read the *Sunday Express*. When I went down to my parents' village in Wiltshire, everyone at the pub would compliment me on my articles, but in London I never met a single *Sunday Express* reader. And after a few years, inevitably, I got itchy feet. I kept applying for other jobs, thinking that as the winner of two British press awards I was bound to be in demand. But I never was – I think the *Sunday Express* was so unfashionable that Fleet Street editors never read it.

But in late 1989 I was having lunch with Ron Hall at the Groucho, when he introduced me to a former *Sunday Times* colleague of his, Ian Jack, who said he was helping to launch a new newspaper, the *Independent on Sunday*. (The *Independent* had been running, very successfully, since 1986, but now it was spawning a Sunday sister, edited by Stephen Glover, with Ian Jack in charge of the Review section.) I said 'Will there be jobs for feature writers?' And he said, 'Maybe. Send me your cuttings.' So I did. But just then the *Sunday Express* sent me to Punta del Este in Uruguay to write about the Whitbread Round-the-World Yacht race. Or actually not about the *race* – heaven forfend – but about the balls, the parties, the celebrations when the yachts arrived. It was supposed to be a great opportunity to see South American high society at play. The *Express* yachting correspondent kept us informed of the race's progress and eventually I got the call – fly out now, the yachts will start arriving in about three days. So I scrambled off to Punta del Este – where I learned that the yachts were still three days offshore, in a dead calm.

They remained that way for something like two weeks. The jet set, who had rushed to Punta del Este when I did, hung around for a day or two and then moved on, never to return. Even the locals lost interest after a while. I sometimes felt I was the only person in Punta del Este who still expected to see sails coming over the horizon. I would stand on the freezing quayside dawn after dawn, *praying* for the sight of a sail, like some poor fisherman's wife whose husband's boat has not come in. And all the time I was going mad with impatience, thinking I was missing my chance of a job at the *Independent on Sunday*. When the yachts did eventually arrive, weeks later in the middle of the night, all the balls and parties had been cancelled, and the only celebration I remember is drinking a lot of Steinlager on the winning New Zealand yacht and hitching a lift on the Rothmans yacht down to Montevideo. And then it was bat out of hell back to England and a very cross David, who had had to do the school run for three weeks instead of the promised four days. I assumed that my chances of joining the new *Independent on Sunday* would have gone.

Success

But no. Luckily the *Independent on Sunday* had been so busy hiring real journalists – foreign correspondents, sports editors, political columnists – they'd completely forgotten about the humble feature-writing job, so it was still open when I got back from Uruguay. I went to see Stephen Glover, the editor, who looked askance at my CV – seven years at *Penthouse*, seven at the *Sunday Express*, two sex books (like so many of the *Independent*'s top brass he was a vicar's son) – but said languidly that Ian Jack and Sebastian Faulks seemed to think my interviews were really very good. The judges of the British press awards thought so too, I told him, given that I'd already won two and fully expected to win more. So, with no great enthusiasm, Glover offered me the job. It meant a huge drop in salary and no car, but by now I was desperate to leave the *Sunday Express*. And it was tremendous fun joining a new newspaper which everyone was talking about. Also I loved the fact that the office was next door to Bunhill Fields cemetery, which has one of the biggest starling roosts in London, so I could hang around the back stairs every sunset watching the birds fly in.

In theory, I was one of a writing team who could turn our hands to anything; in practice, I started doing interviews from the day I arrived and made that my speciality.

We did dummy runs for about two months before the paper was launched so I assembled a good backlog of interviews for Stephen Glover to choose from. In the very first issue he ran an interview I did with John Aspinall in which – I always believe – Aspinall admitted to having seen Lord Lucan after he murdered his nanny. But the wording was slightly ambiguous and nobody else seemed to read it as I did, so that first interview passed without comment. But some of my interviews over the next few weeks attracted huge attention, especially an attack on Melvyn Bragg and an interview with Richard Harris in which I commented on his strange habit of rummaging about in his tracksuit bottom. Suddenly, at the age of forty-six, I was an 'overnight success'. People started calling me Demon Barber and writing hot-under-the-collar articles about whether such 'aggressive' interviewing should be allowed. I found all the fuss very odd because I'd been writing similar interviews for the *Sunday Express* for years, but suddenly I was characterised as this mega-bitch hatchet-woman who stitched everyone up. I worried that it would stop people agreeing to be interviewed by me. It probably did stop some, but to others it seemed to act as a spur – they felt it was a badge of courage to take me on.

(I'm still quite bemused by the Demon Barber reputation. I think it arises from the fact that readers remember the hatchet jobs more than they remember the friendly pieces. But whether this is because I write them better, or because of general *Schadenfreude*, I never know. The interviews *I* remember from the *Independent on Sunday* are the more thoughtful ones I did with Rudolf Nureyev, Roald Dahl, Muriel Spark, but they got less attention. The same thing happened again at the *Observer* – it was the hatchet jobs on, say, Harriet Harman, Marianne Faithfull or John Prescott that readers seemed to remember.)

That first year on the *Independent on Sunday* – 1990 – was my glory year, when I won another press award, and also a *What the Papers Say* award, and had almost non-stop attention. Suddenly all sorts of people wanted to meet me, strange dining societies from the Inns of Court to the Royal Naval College at Greenwich were asking me to grace them with my presence, clubs were offering me complimentary membership, the Oxford and Cambridge Unions wanted me to speak in their debates. I accepted a few of these invitations but soon realised that I found such occasions depressing, and would come back feeling obscurely dejected. At first I couldn't work out why but then I realised – all these people who wanted to meet me were clearly disappointed when they *did* meet me. Whatever they were hoping for, I wasn't it. Partly, I suppose, it was my age. When the launch issue of the *Independent on Sunday* was going to press, Stephen Glover had said, 'We'd better give you a picture byline – do you have a photograph of yourself?' I did indeed, a very nice photo that I'd been using for years at the *Sunday Express*. Unfortunately it was ten years old and the intervening years had not been kind so the photograph gave a highly misleading impression of my looks. But there was more than that – people expected me to talk as I write, i.e. crisply and decisively, whereas actually I am a terrible waffler and of course burdened with an elocution accent. If I could communicate only by words on a page, how much more satisfactory I would be!

My brush with fame was minuscule and short-lived – it lasted a matter of months – but it gave me some sympathy with the problems of real fame. It is extremely disconcerting to meet people who think they know you when you have no idea who they are. But they often talk with such familiarity, as if they *really* know you, that you feel they must be old friends or colleagues whom you have somehow, unforgivably, forgotten. I suppose that really famous people must get used to it – but then getting used to it must cut them off from normal people and make it more difficult, or even impossible, to form ordinary friendships across the fame divide. Jonathan Ross once told me about what he calls 'the fame nod' – the way famous people will nod to each other across a crowded room, establishing rapport. He says that the public always assume that all famous people know each other, so they never get properly introduced: the nod is a way of saying, 'I know who you are and I expect you know who I am too.'

(In recent years I've had another little taste of, not fame, but face recognition when I've appeared on a long-running television series called *Grumpy Old Women*. I found that if I went shopping in Crouch End the morning after one of these programmes had been transmitted, quite a few strangers would nod and smile at me in the street. If I went the following day, I might get one or two nods. But by day three there'd be no signs of recognition – television memories are that short.)

Working on the *Independent on Sunday* was tremendous fun at the beginning because I had some great colleagues – Ian Jack, Zoë Heller, Sebastian Faulks, Blake Morrison, Allison Pearson, Nick Cohen, Simon Garfield, Michael Fathers – but the circulation soon began dropping like a stone. There was general dissatisfaction with Stephen Glover, the editor, and endless plots to oust him. I didn't object to the plots – what I objected to was not being invited to join them. But then I was a woman. In all my years on *Penthouse* and the *Sunday Express* I had never for a minute known what it was to suffer sexual discrimination (nor have I since), but the *Independent on Sunday* was run by an entirely male cabal who clearly regarded women as second-class citizens. They would occasionally invite me or Zoë to conference if there were television cameras about but were normally quite content to have all-male meetings at which they would solemnly discuss the question 'What do women want?' I remember once Peter Wilby, deputy editor, popped his head out of conference to ask me 'What do women think of Maastricht?' before going back to tell his colleagues, 'She says not interested.' The trouble with feeling discriminated against, I found, is that it is cumulative and corrosive: you start becoming more and more 'sensitive' to perceived slights till you develop a really heavy chip on your shoulder. I would go home and rant to David about patriarchy and male chauvinism while he stirred the risotto and asked whether I wanted *poires Hélènes* to follow. It was a crazy situation and made me eager to escape the *Independent on Sunday* for my own sanity.

Escape came eventually in the portly shape of Graydon Carter. In 1993 I was having lunch at the Groucho Club (as so often in those days) when someone told me that Graydon had just been appointed editor of *Vanity Fair* in succession to Tina Brown. I knew him slightly – he had bought several of my *Independent on Sunday* interviews to run in the *New York Observer*, which he edited, and at his request I had called to see him when I was in New York. He was a besotted Anglophile with an absurd collection of English country-house bric-a-brac in his office – old cricket bats, snowshoes and sepia photographs of rowing teams – but I loved his bonhomie and wit. As soon as I heard he'd gone to *Vanity Fair*, I thought, I wonder if he'll offer me a job? Sure enough, the phone call came that very afternoon.

He offered me a contract for a quite fabulous amount of money. The only drawback was that he wanted me to move to New York. I said I couldn't – David worked in London, the girls were still at school – but Graydon compromised and said I could remain in London provided I pop over to New York at regular intervals. My idea of a regular interval was once a year whereas his, it turned out, was more like once a month, but actually that was the least of our problems. The main one was that I was just not cut out to be an American journalist. In England, I could phone my editor and say 'Do you want an interview with X?' and get an immediate yes or no. At *Vanity Fair* I had to 'pitch ideas' and then go through layers of editors, all of whom asked what my 'angle' was going to be. I have always deeply hated and resented this question. If you have an angle on someone, it means you have already decided what to write before you meet, so you really might as well not bother interviewing them. But the *Vanity Fair* editors seemed to expect almost a synopsis of the interview before it took place. Also, getting ideas past this incredible bureaucracy meant they were often months out of date by the time they were approved.

Then there were the fact-checkers. Of course I'd read *Bright Lights, Big City* and knew what fact-checking entailed, but I still didn't realise what an incredible palaver I was letting myself in for. The weirdest example came when I was writing a profile of P. D. James and said something about her spending the weekend in Salisbury. Back came the fact-checkers. What was this place Sall-is-burry? Well, it's a cathedral city in Wiltshire, about 100 miles west of London. What was my source for saying that? Well, as a matter of fact, my parents live near there. That, it turned out, was not a source. I had to find an 'accredited' guidebook that said where Salisbury was. Of course it wasn't difficult, but what was infuriating was that they then put a great chunk from the guidebook into my article so that P. D. James spent the weekend in 'Salisbury, a city founded in medieval times in the county of Wiltshire and famous for having the highest cathedral spire – 404 feet – in England.' It was madness, but it happened again and again – huge wodges of irrelevant fact would suddenly appear in the middle of my paragraphs, completely ruining the flow.

Another difficulty was that *Vanity Fair* writers were supposed to live a sort of *Vanity Fair* lifestyle, mixing with 'movers and shakers' and attending 'important' parties. Once I was actually flown over to New York and put up at the Royalton for three days to attend a *Vanity Fair* anniversary bash, which was huge fun but somewhat baffling – what was I *doing* there? But Graydon was/is a great believer in the values of parties and has proved his point with his annual post-Oscars celebration, which has become by far the hottest social ticket in Hollywood. Unfortunately, I was slow to recognize that a Graydon invitation counted as a three-line whip. The only time I seriously annoyed him – far more than when I screwed up a cover story, of which more later – was when I said I couldn't attend a dinner for Lord Snowdon because I was interviewing Michael Caine early the next morning and needed an early night. Most British editors would have been impressed by my dedication but not Graydon. 'You're only *interviewing* him,' he snorted, and I didn't like to say 'But that's what you pay me for.' In retrospect, I think I was far too priggish, but I came from the old Grub Street tradition whereby hacks were meant to be pariahs who would rather chew their own arms off than hobnob with celebs.

But the major difficulty in working for *Vanity Fair* was that none of the big Hollywood names Graydon wanted me to interview would agree to see me. They had a (probably well-founded) distrust of British journalists, especially British journalists who bore the nickname Demon Barber, so I spent a lot of time twiddling my thumbs. Huge Fedex packages would arrive almost daily with 'research material' and books I 'might like to think about', but interviews came there none. To make matters worse I was not allowed to write for anyone else, so I became quite neurotic under the weight of all this leisure. Relax, enjoy, I told myself, but the more I said it, the more I fretted. I was not cut out for lotus-eating and could never reconcile myself to being paid an awful lot of money for doing nothing.

Eventually Graydon phoned and said they'd got me an interview with the film actor Nick Nolte, and it would be the cover story and Annie Leibovitz would do the photographs. The interview was scheduled for a Friday evening, at Nolte's house in Malibu, so I flew out to Los Angeles, spent an enjoyable few days 'preparing' by the pool at the Peninsula, and was driven out to Nolte's house on Friday evening. The house itself was very dark, I remember, a bit sinister, but Nolte seemed friendly enough and when I left after about three hours, I thought the interview had gone pretty well. I checked the tapes – they were fine – and went to bed happily, looking forward to meeting Annie Leibovitz the next morning.

I was woken by one of *Vanity Fair*'s editors phoning from New York to ask 'What happened?' Apparently Nolte's publicist had called Graydon in the night to say the photo shoot was off, all future co-operation with *Vanity Fair* was off, because I'd upset Nolte so badly. What? But he was perfectly friendly when I left. I still to this day don't know what happened. I played the tape to Graydon and he didn't know either. Maybe I hadn't been as deferential as you are meant to be with a Hollywood star, but Nolte hadn't seemed upset at the time. Graydon behaved heroically, telling me I mustn't blame myself, but it must have been a blow for him, losing his cover story at the last minute, and having to tell Annie Leibovitz to turn round and go home. And it meant my career as a Hollywood interviewer was effectively over before it had begun – Nolte's publicist, Pat Kingsley, in those days controlled all the major stars and she was never going to let me loose on one of them again. Graydon nobly kept me on contract for two years but we both knew my future at *Vanity Fair* was zilch.

And in truth I was quite glad to get back to being over-worked and underpaid, in grubby old Grub Street, after the limousine luxury of *Vanity Fair*. I worked briefly for the *Sunday Times*, which was horrible, and then more enjoyably for the *Telegraph* Magazine, but didn't really settle down till I joined the *Observer* in 1996. When I first arrived, it was a bit chaotic because they'd changed editor about four times in as many years, and there were all these different strata of staff from different editorships, but once Roger Alton took over it was fine. He was the most inspiring and enthusiastic editor I have ever worked for – when he left, at Christmas 2007, we had a whole week of leaving parties when all the staff including me stood around in tears applauding him. Editors who can inspire such affection are rare – the ones usually cited are Kelvin MacKenzie at the *Sun* and Harold Evans at the *Sunday Times* – and I feel privileged to have worked for one. But his successor, John Mulholland, looks pretty promising too.

Since joining the *Observer*, I've won two more British press awards, and was particularly pleased to get one in

2002 which meant I could say that I'd won press awards over three decades – or better still, over two millennia. I know it is appallingly naff to boast about awards but I adore them – not least because they serve to reassure my parents that I won't necessarily get the sack tomorrow. (Still waiting for that rainy day, they keep telling me I can always go back to shorthand typing.) What I love about the *Observer* – apart from my dear colleagues – is that it has always given me great freedom in choosing my subjects and let me run the whole gamut from, say, Kerry Katona to Gerry Adams. There is always a danger for an interviewer that you will be cast as either a lightweight or a heavyweight, but I have managed to skip fairly nimbly between the two. And that for me is the whole joy and point of interviewing – to celebrate the *variety* of the human race.

Best of all, the *Observer* has let me develop my burgeoning interest in interviewing artists. I'd always felt that artists were terribly under-interviewed compared to, say, actors, and this was certainly true until the mid-Nineties, when the YBAs came along. But luckily I joined the *Observer* just when there was this eye-catching new generation of artists, led by Damien Hirst and Tracey Emin, who were more than happy to play with journalists. I love interviewing artists because I always feel I am doing something *useful*, which is trying to find a way of talking about art that isn't the usual impenetrable art theory bollocks but isn't *Daily Mail* philistinism either. It slightly reminds me of the early days of writing about sex for *Penthouse* – there are so many *bad* ways of talking about art, you feel

131

that if you can find a good way, you are laying stepping stones across the quagmire for others to follow. Another bonus is that some of the artists I've interviewed have become good friends and enlivened my social life to no end. Going to the Venice Biennale with Tracey Emin was one of the all-time fun experiences of my life, though a Suffolk weekend with Sarah Lucas was a close runner-up. I was also thrilled to be asked to be a Turner Prize juror in 2006 – it is something I like to boast about, along with my five British press awards. I am no more an art expert than I was ever a sex expert or a Victorian natural history expert, but I am more than happy to pick up any claims to expertise that come my way.

Disaster

So this is where I'd got to circa 2000. I was in my mid-fifties, pretty confident, pretty happy, in truth pretty smug. I loved my job, I loved my life. We had raised a family, we had bought a big house in Highgate and paid off the mortgage, the daughters were at university. My parents, long retired, were living in a beautiful village, Ebbesborne Wake, in Wiltshire where, despite Dad being blind and Mum arthritic, they seemed able to cope on their own. David's mother had died and his father had sold Little Haseley and moved into Oxford, but he too seemed able to cope. David – by now disenchanted with the Poly, which had moved to Harrow and renamed itself the University of Westminster – could afford to take early retirement and go back to painting. He rented an Acme studio in the old Pears factory in Hackney, and I waved him off after breakfast every morning and went up to my study to work. We had achieved the future we'd dreamed of all those years ago in Stockwell – David painting, me writing, free of money worries, free to run our own lives. I felt we had come through.

The beginning of the end came in the summer of 2001 when we were staying with a friend in Gloucestershire and David woke in the night and found he couldn't pee. It was the symptom he had always dreaded, the one he had a hypochondriac's encyclopaedic knowledge of, the first sign, he believed, of prostate cancer. I drove him to Cheltenham Hospital, David keening with pain, me mowing down foxes, rabbits, rats, stoats, as we raced over the moonlit hills to Cheltenham. In A & E, men covered in blood were shouting and fighting while a nurse asked about David's symptoms and wrote down 'Retention.' He was seen by an exhausted junior doctor who confirmed between yawns that yes, David had an enlarged prostate, but no, it didn't mean cancer. Many men in their fifties, she told him, suffered from an enlarged prostate – it could easily be treated with drugs. She fitted a catheter, drained his bladder, gave him some pills, and told him to consult his GP on Monday.

The GP prescribed pills that solved the problem, so much so that David almost stopped worrying about it. The only reminder was that he had to go for a blood test every three months to check his PSA. On 16 October 2002 he went for his regular blood test at the Whittington hospital – and was called back for another test, and then another. By this stage we were expecting bad news – bad news about his prostate. But when David saw the haematologist on 25 October, he came back with news so bad we really couldn't comprehend it: they thought he had chronic leukaemia. He would have to have a bone marrow test and a spleen test to confirm it. But the doctor told David – meaning to reassure him – that he could live for another ten years.

Ten years! David was then fifty-eight; neither of us had ever doubted that he would live into his nineties like his father. He didn't smoke, barely drank, took loads of exercise and looked absurdly young. On the rare occasions I tried to imagine my own death, David was always at the bedside, holding my hand. But now, for the first time, I had to contemplate the idea that I might outlive David, that I might one day be a widow. But still – ten years down the line. How could I imagine that? And how was I supposed to comport myself in the meantime? Was I suddenly supposed to be the doting wife, sticking to my husband's side, tending his every whim? For ten days maybe, but not for ten years. Anyway, it would drive him mad, never mind me.

I said tentatively, and hoping for the answer no, 'Perhaps I should give up work and we could travel to India, Australia, all those places you've never been?' He laughed and said, 'I never want to go abroad again. I hate abroad.' This was as much of a shock as the ten years. He always loved abroad, I thought – all our married life I'd felt guilty that my work often took me abroad and his never did. And every year I would book us a foreign holiday – resenting it – because I thought it was unfair that I had all those stamps in my passport and he didn't. 'Since when did you hate abroad?' 'Oh, years now,' he said casually. I felt as outraged as if he'd told me he'd been having an affair for years now. But perhaps this is what goes wrong with long marriages – you state your opinions, your likes and dislikes, at the beginning and then forget to mention when they change.

'But *you* go abroad,' he said. 'I won't stop you.'

'But I never want to go abroad!'

135

'Yes, you do, you like it.'

'No I don't, I hate it.'

'But you're always going.'

'But I always hate it.'

Thus my very first attempt to play the self-sacrificing wife resulted in a blazing row within minutes and I thought, 'Well sod that, I won't try again.' Which was fine, because at least now we could carry on as normal but with the advantage of knowing something we'd inexplicably missed knowing for years – that neither of us ever wanted to go abroad. He said we'd go to Cornwall in the spring as we always did, and then make the usual rounds of friends in Norfolk, Yorkshire, Scotland, the Peak District, but for our main holiday, instead of going abroad, we'd take a big house in the Lake District and have friends to stay.

So I spent hours on the internet ostensibly looking for holiday houses in the Lake District, while actually reading all the dozens of leukaemia websites. Very few of them said anything about life expectancy – but the ones that did suggested five years rather than ten. I felt grateful yet again that David had never mastered the internet. Rosie meanwhile was printing out some of the more anodyne leukaemia websites – I noticed that she was careful to leave out all the bad bits.

David's next appointment was with a top haematologist and, armed with knowledge from the internet, I told him to find out whether he had hairy-cell leukaemia or the other sort. He came back saying he didn't have leukaemia at all – he had something called myelofibrosis which was a disease of the bone marrow. 'Oh, that's good news,' I said – surely it was better to have something you'd never heard of than something that was known to kill people? Yes, he agreed, it was good news – so we rang all our friends and said, 'Good news! It's not leukaemia after all.'

Or rather, I rang all our friends. David, from the beginning, thought it was wrong of me to tell people about his illness. He would have kept it a secret from everyone, even our daughters, if he could. This had been a bone of contention throughout our marriage – his habit of secrecy, mine of disclosure. He couldn't see why I *needed* to confide in friends; I couldn't see why he *needed* to keep secrets. He thought I was a blabbermouth; I thought he was paranoid. I told him I liked talking to friends, and there wasn't much point in talking to them if I wasn't going to tell them things. I often noticed when I interviewed people that they would say, 'Well, everyone has skeletons in their closets', but actually I could never think of a single toe-bone of a skeleton in mine, not because I'd led a virtuous life, but because I'd never kept anything secret for more than ten minutes. I think keeping secrets is a strain, almost a sickness. It queers your relationships, means you must always live in fear of being 'exposed'. And whereas generally I thought David's habit of secrecy was a man thing, and my habit of blabbing was a woman thing – not that he was wrong and I was right, but just an innate difference of temperament – I felt absolutely sure over his illness that it was *right* to tell our friends, and that it was unthinkable not to, and therefore I went ahead and told everyone before he had a chance to stop me. Everyone, that is, except his family – I accepted that it was up to him, not me, to tell his brothers and father at a time of his choosing.

What made this period all so strange was that David was told he had a mortal disease while he had no obvious symptoms at all – he looked perfectly fit until the day he went into hospital. The only concrete symptom the doctor could point to was that he had an enlarged spleen, and David agreed, when the doctor showed him where his spleen was, that yes, there was a sort of lump there and sometimes he'd noticed his waistband getting tighter. As the months went on, the lump got larger and I could sometimes see it bulging through his shirt. The only other slight sign was an occasional red rash on his cheeks which the doctor said was 'insignificant'. It was very significant to David – he hated anything that impaired his looks.

But yet, in a way, there *had* been symptoms – I had noticed for the past two or three years that David was finally ageing. Not ageing dramatically, not looking like a man in his late fifties, but he had aged from looking about thirty throughout his forties, to suddenly looking maybe forty-five. There were a few lines on his cheeks, some new hollows and stringy bits in his neck, the odd liver spot on his hands, and the faintest beginnings of a tonsure hole in his thick dark hair. I used to point these out with some glee – I *longed* for him to age a bit – I told him that I didn't mind people mistaking him for my toy boy but I resented it when they mistook him for my son. I was only ten days older than David, but at some point soon after forty I turned middle-aged whereas he never did. But for the last two or three years, I realised, he'd been catching up – and catching up fast. It wasn't just the bald spot, the mottled hands, but more a tiredness – the creaky way he heaved himself up from the sofa, the way sometimes he put his elbows on the table and sunk his head in his hands as if the weight of carrying it was too much. And I noticed he was ageing in other ways – he hated pop music, he grumbled about people using mobile phones on the train. I used to think sometimes, 'You look so young still, but mentally you are older than me.'

Of course I read up myelofibrosis on the internet and learned it was a progressive furring-up of the bone marrow, but again, as with leukaemia, there was little detail about life expectancy – though one site mentioned four years. That was the worst – other sites tended to say five to ten years if they said anything at all. But still, while our friends were still congratulating him on not having leukaemia, it occurred to me that maybe, just maybe, myelofibrosis was worse.

He went to see the head haematologist at the Whittington who told him that the only cure for myelofibrosis was a bone-marrow transplant – but that the top age for bone-marrow transplants was fifty-five. However, he said, he would refer him to Dr MacKinnon, the head of bone-marrow transplants at UCH. From then on Dr MacKinnon became our god – on his say-so David's life depended. David came back from seeing him with good news, and bad. The good news was that he agreed David could have a transplant, despite being over-age, provided they could find a suitable donor. But the risks of fatality were quite high – 10 per cent if the donor was a sibling, 30 per cent if a stranger. The bad news was that, without it, David had only 'two good years' to live. Moreover, he should have the transplant as soon as possible because otherwise the fibrosis would be too advanced for it to work. Since then, I've wondered a lot about those two good years. I wish I'd asked: would there have been two good years, and then say two goodish, and two or three not so good – I mean how long, actually, would he have lived? But David didn't even ask those questions – he had total trust in Dr MacKinnon. He would have the transplant; he would be cured; hooray!

Dr MacKinnon's decision was influenced by the fact that David had two brothers, either of whom could be donors. He said that obviously they would need to come to UCH for extensive testing beforehand, but that the actual bone-marrow donation process was no big deal. I had imagined it entailed carving a sort of osso buco lump out of a limb and somehow grafting it onto David's bone but, on the contrary, it was just a needle in the arm, hardly more than donating blood. Charles, David's elder brother, was inconveniently in Papua New Guinea visiting his son who was doing VSO there, but Luke, his younger brother, lived just down the road. If it had been me, I'd have run to Luke's house the minute I got back from the hospital, but David waited several days before going to see him. I wondered why he was so reluctant to go; David told me not to nag.

Meanwhile we read 'the book'. The book was a substantial plastic-bound manual called *Your bone-marrow transplant*. It was a model of clarity – and, reading it, how I longed for obfuscation! David actually shook the first

140

time he read it. I could never read it through – I would open a page at random and put it down, feeling sick. It listed all the drugs he would have to take and their terrible side effects – nausea, hair loss, hives, mouth ulcers, diarrhoea, debilitation. Basically, he had to take a long course of toxic drugs to kill his own immune system before they could introduce the donor bone marrow, and there was a very dangerous week in the middle of the transplant when he would have no immunity at all.

Luke went for tests as soon as David told him, but we had to wait two weeks for the results. Cruelly, on a Friday UCH rang to say they had got the results and what was Luke's phone number to tell him? He was out filming all day (he is a cameraman), his mobile was switched off. Oh please, please, I cried, tell us the results. But protocol demanded that they must tell the donor first, and they never got hold of Luke that Friday so we spent the weekend in suspense. Or rather, I spent it in suspense while David, again, was eerily patient. 'Don't you want to know,' I raged, 'whether you're going to *live* or *die*? I'd be just a *bit* curious myself! How can you fake this stupid indifference?' I think actually it wasn't indifference but pessimism: he fully expected bad news, as he always expected bad news; he wanted another two days of hope.

On Monday, we got the results – Luke was a perfect match, the bone-marrow transplant could go ahead. But, they said, they still wanted to test Charles as 'back up'. This meant waiting two more weeks till Charles returned from Papua New Guinea. David again seemed quite happy to wait, while I was climbing the walls with impatience. Why did they need to bother with Charles? He might not want to be a donor – he was diabetic and had his own health problems – also he lived in Hampshire, so it was a slog for him to come to UCH. But when he eventually got back to England and David told him, he was fine, and trotted off to UCH to be tested. He was found to be a perfect match too – in fact he was mysteriously deemed to be an even more perfect match than Luke. So he would be the prime donor, and Luke the 'back-up', whatever that meant.

Only at this point did David say, laughing, 'So they *are* my brothers after all!' I was too shocked to speak. We had been married for over thirty years and only now did I discover that David had always thought what I had always thought – that maybe he was not his father's son. It was quite a reasonable suspicion because David was dark and Jewish-looking like his mother, whereas his brothers were blond and English-looking like their father. Also he was born in 1944, when his father was away fighting the war so it was not impossible, I thought, that Leonora had had a fling in his absence. I remember when I first met David's family, I wondered if I dared broach this suspicion to David, but I never did, and then of course forgot about it until what had been a question of mild historic interest became suddenly urgent in the face of the bone-marrow tests. But obviously David had been worrying about it all along – that was why he was so slow to ask Luke to get tested.

What a lot I was learning after thirty years of marriage! I now knew that my husband hated abroad, and had suspected all his life that he was not his father's son.

I've always been a great believer in the essential unknow-ability of other people, but it seems a bit bad not to know such things about your husband. But there was a deep substratum of emotion connected with his family that I had never understood – childhood sludge that had lain almost undisturbed throughout our marriage suddenly swirled and sent up gloopy bubbles from the murk. Why was he so reluctant to tell his father about his illness? He said it was because he didn't want to worry Maurice, but I sometimes wondered if it was because he was afraid Maurice would not be worried *enough*. He put off telling Maurice from month to month, and said what was the point of telling him? But then, I always thought, what was the point of *not* telling him? He would have to know eventually. David couldn't disappear into hospital for weeks (we were told six weeks minimum) without his father noticing.

Ever since his mother died, David had been in the habit of visiting his father in Oxford at least once a fort-night. They had lunch together and visited churches or went for walks in the Chilterns. Occasionally I went too, but David seemed to prefer going alone. But increas-ingly, as the weeks wore on, I noticed that he seemed to come back from these visits with a heavier and heavier load of resentment – he complained that Maurice was completely self-obsessed, and only talked about his own ailments, his dodgy knee, his occasional toothache. David seemed to think that Maurice should have some-how 'known' that he was ill. But how could Maurice know unless David told him? I urged him again and again to tell his father, but he said it would be better to tell him when we knew the date of the transplant, when all the uncertainties were resolved. And, he told me, I had no right to interfere – it was *his* illness, *his* father. So we spent an uneasy family Christmas, with everyone, even Luke's teenage children, knowing about David but Maurice still in the dark, still talking about his dodgy knee, his twinges of toothache. David accused me of rolling my eyes at dinner. Maybe I did.

A few days later, when we were staying with friends in Yorkshire for New Year, my parents rang to say that their cottage had been flooded, for the second time that winter. I drove down to Wiltshire to collect them and then back to London. I got so bored with them yakking on about their flooding that I snapped, 'Listen, I have something important to tell you. Mum, put your hearing aid in. I SAID PUT YOUR HEARING AID IN. David has a very serious illness. He has to have a bone-marrow transplant. They said there's a ten per cent chance it will kill him.' That shut them up and we spent the rest of the drive in silence. I felt quite pleased with myself.

Punishment came a few days later when my father announced that, in view of David's illness, they had decided to sell their cottage. (Don't look for any rhyme or reason – we are in Dick Barber territory.) He was going to ring an estate agent immediately and put it on the market. This was in January, when the cottage was still ankle-deep in water, with sandbags at the door, looking as bad as it was possible for a chocolate-box thatched cottage to look. I urged patience – couldn't he wait just a couple of months, till the water had receded, till the spring bulbs and apple blossom came out, till the cottage looked beautiful again instead of bedraggled? No, no – no time like the present. My father's insane impatience was an exact counterpoint to David's insane patience – and I was driven demented by them both. I tried an appeal to pity – 'Dad, I've got enough on my plate right now, can't you just wait till David's sorted out?' 'No, no, can't hang about' – and within a week he'd sold the cottage to a passing builder for £50,000 less than the estate agent said it was worth.

Of course he had not thought about where they would live but said airily, 'We'll rent somewhere. Or we could stay in a hotel.'

'In London?' I trembled.

'Good God no, not London,' he roared. 'We couldn't live in London with all that noise.' This was delivered at his usual shouting-from-a-ship-in-high-seas volume, then, for my mother's benefit, 'I SAID WE COULDN'T LIVE IN LONDON WITH ALL THE NOISE.'

'OF COURSE NOT,' she screeched. 'ALL THAT TRAFFIC!' Actually they could have lived in the middle of Spaghetti Junction without hearing a thing but fine, London was too noisy – and a weight off my mind. Now all I had to do was find them a place to rent. I trawled the internet and rang up estate agents, but found that landlords are not too keen on letting cottages to couples in their late eighties, one of whom is blind and the other arthritic. But meanwhile their cleaner had somehow found them a smart newbuilt house in Nunton, near Salisbury, and, by the time they told me, they'd already

145

signed the lease and organised the move.

David went down to help on moving day and wept when they drove away from Ebbesborne Wake – he loved the place. My parents never gave it a backward glance. They had lived there for twenty years but off with the old, on with the new. Months later they proudly showed me an estate agent's ad for the cottage – except that it was now called a 'Lodge' and marooned in a sea of gravel, with no trace of a mossed cottage tree or rambling rose anywhere. The side lawn where I counted the fritillaries every year was covered with paving. 'They've done it up real nice,' my parents said proudly.

And then another disaster out of the blue – our dear friend Richard died. His partner Hugh found him dead in bed when he took him his morning tea. Hugh rang me distraught and I turned up on his Hampstead doorstep just as the police were arriving – apparently they have to investigate any sudden death. They were polite but I suddenly realised why civil partnerships are necessary – they addressed all their questions to me as if Hugh did not exist. I said, 'But Hugh is his flatmate, he's lived with Richard for twenty-five years.' But still with every question, they turned to me – When did Richard last visit his GP? Had he complained of any illness? – and I would ask Hugh and relay the answer to them. And the police insisted on phoning Richard's brother to ask what arrangements he wanted to make for the 'disposal of the remains' after the autopsy and again Richard's brother kept saying, 'Well what does Hugh want?' But in the eyes of the police Hugh had no status at all.

They took Richard's body away in an unmarked gray van. The autopsy revealed what we expected – that he died of a heart attack. He was buried on a beautiful spring day in the churchyard of his brother's village in Sussex. Getting dressed for the funeral, David found that he could no longer do up the jacket of his best suit over his bulging spleen. At the service he said to me lightly, 'I like a traditional church funeral, all the old hymns,' and I nodded and said yes of course, I agreed.

Shortly afterwards, we went to a solicitor and made our wills, leaving everything to each other. We had never discussed doing it before. But somehow Richard's death made it all right to raise these taboo subjects – the will, the funeral – and I thought that, of all the many favours Richard had done us, he did almost the biggest in death. It meant that David, Rosie, Theo and I were able to weep together at his funeral and talk about what hymns we liked and what readings. Keen atheists though we were, we agreed a church service was best.

At last all the tests were complete and the hospital fixed a date for David to have his spleen removed – apparently this was essential because otherwise the spleen would make competing platelets and mess up his transplant. Then he would have six to eight weeks to recover before he went into UCH. We arranged to go to Cornwall for Easter, and then to the Lake District just before the splenectomy, so he would be as fit as possible from all those long walks. At this point David finally told his father, who was, predictably, hurt that David hadn't told him before. He asked about David's operation and then went back to complaining about his dodgy knee, his twanging teeth.

A couple of weeks before Easter, David went for his regular prostate test – and was told he had prostate cancer. He had moved up a notch on the prostate scale, which was the point at which they stopped talking about an enlarged prostate and started talking about cancer. If he went up another notch, it meant the cancer had become 'aggressive' and might 'break out'. So did that mean his transplant would not now go ahead? After all, they had made an exception in agreeing to treat him when he was over the age limit; it would be an even bigger exception to agree to treat him when he had cancer. The great god MacKinnon referred him to a whole new set of doctors at the Royal Free who would have to decide what to do about his cancer.

So we went on holiday to Cornwall with this terrible uncertainty. If they treated his prostate – and even if they cured it completely – he would probably be too late to have the transplant. Or if they went ahead with the transplant, it would mean leaving the cancer to grow, unchecked, for however long it would take his bone marrow to recover. At this point, for the first time, I began to despair. I thought, he's going to be in and out of hospital for the rest of his life – why not just say to hell with treatment, let's go for two good years. But when I very tentatively floated this idea, David seemed so upset I never mentioned it again.

But, for all the uncertainty, we were closer on this holiday that we had been for years – it felt like a return to the happiest early days of our marriage and young parenthood. We walked the same cliff paths, admired the same wild flowers and reminisced about our first holidays in Cornwall when Rosie and Theo were babies. How energetic we were then! We would think nothing of walking from Coverack to Cadgwith over the huge cliffs of Black Head with Rosie on David's shoulders, Theo in a sling on my tummy, all of us so thrilled to be in Cornwall, so enchanted by the cliffs and the view. We were terribly poor, and terribly happy. The rot set in a few years later when I suffered a string of slipped discs, which meant I could never walk long distances again. By then I was back at work, so we could afford much more luxurious foreign holidays, in villas with pools and maids, and those holidays were fun too, but we were never such a self-contained little family again.

That Easter in Cornwall gave us a much-needed chance to remember why we'd fallen in love in the first place. Our marriage had become like a neglected allotment where no one had bothered to do any weeding for a long time. But in Cornwall we found ourselves going back to the early days, delighting in each other's knowledge (David's of flowers, mine of birds), laughing at each other's fears (David's of heights, mine of cows), holding hands along the cliffs. I thought: this is how our marriage should be from now on. Maybe I could even give up work and we could move to Cornwall? David laughed when I suggested it – 'You'd be bored rigid within days!' But he seemed happy that I'd made the offer. And all the time, in the background, in the small hours, in bed, we were making these secret calculations – cancer, transplant, transplant, cancer – how long, O lord, how long?

After Cornwall, there was a rush of hospital appointments – scans for his prostate cancer, tests on his spleen, tests on his blood, one day good news, one day bad, a whole new cast of doctors at the Royal Free as well as the bone-marrow lot at UCH, the spleen lot at the Middlesex and the haematology lot at the Whittington. David never explicitly gave up going to his studio but there was hardly a day when he didn't have a hospital appointment. And occasionally he would say things – 'I can't face another biopsy' or 'I don't want to take pills that make me fat' – that made me wonder if he realised what a long, ghastly business the transplant would be. Eventually the Royal Free oncologists and the UCH transplant team somehow decided between them that he would have the transplant first and then worry about the prostate cancer later. There was a chance, they said, that the transplant would arrest the cancer. So finally we had the dates – splenectomy in May, transplant in July – which gave an illusion of certainty to his future.

I delivered him to the Middlesex for his splenectomy on 18 May. He had never spent a night in hospital before and was appalled by the lack of privacy, the idea that he would have to talk to strangers just because they happened to be in the next bed. I told him off for being such an uptight Old Etonian and in the end, of course, he got quite fond of his neighbours. But he never stopped being shocked that they didn't read. He could lose himself in Saint-Simon – they couldn't even manage the *Sun*.

The operation went well and left only a two-inch scar, though apparently David's spleen was so enormous the surgeon had it pickled as an exhibit. My birthday fell the day after his operation and I thought David was bound to forget, but in fact he had made me a beautiful sketchbook of small abstract paintings – the best present he ever gave me, which he must have been working on for months. He was home in time for *his* birthday ten days later, which we celebrated with lobster and champagne. He was a bit tireder, a bit thinner – he lost half a stone in hospital – but looked fine. The only bad news was that his blood platelet count was extremely high and he had to inject himself to prevent clotting. He had been warned this might happen, but still it was frightening, learning to use these syringes – a reminder that something mysterious and foul was still going on.

He was told to spend the two months between his splenectomy and transplant building his strength and putting on weight, which he happily did. A week before his transplant we went to a friend's son's wedding in Northern Ireland, and David was on brilliant form, singing, joking, dancing the night away. When he told friends that he was going into hospital for a bone-marrow transplant they simply didn't believe him. The following Sunday we drank champagne and sat in the garden till the sun set. It was the start of England's longest, hottest summer for a century – and David's last day at home. Next morning, Monday, 7 July, I delivered him to UCH.

The sad thing, reading my diary, is how the months of diagnosis and waiting and indecision before David's transplant tended to push us onto separate paths. In the diary, I find myself increasingly describing him like 'the patient' – noting his odd moods, his sudden furies, his 'twitchiness', but seeing these as symptoms rather than real feelings. Inevitably he began to seem self-obsessed, always talking about his illness, and the next hospital appointment. And the appointments came thicker and faster as the months went on, throwing up a whole cast of doctors who were only names to me – Panos, the Cypriot haematologist he revered; Miller, the urologist he loathed because he stuck his finger up his bottom; and the all-powerful MacKinnon, who decided whether he could have the transplant or not. I never met any of them – David never suggested that I should come on these hospital appointments and nor did I. I don't know whether it was in his mind but it was certainly in mine that perhaps if I accompanied him, it would remind the doctors that he was older than he looked and therefore less eligible for a transplant. Also we both agreed that I would tend to say the wrong thing, ask awkward questions, as I always did – though in retrospect that is exactly what I wish I had done.

Until David went into hospital, he was always the believer, I the sceptic. I thought he was too trusting of the doctors and their do-or-die certainties, their neat percentages. I noticed as the months wore on, that all these supposedly straightforward treatments carried some collateral damage – no one warned him, for instance, that after his splenectomy he would have to inject himself to prevent clotting and take antibiotics for the rest of his life. But then – inexplicably – as soon as he went into UCH I stopped worrying entirely. The fact that there was a whole wing devoted to bone-marrow transplants, the fact that the doctors and nurses all seemed so cheerful and competent, made me think, oh, it's perfectly routine. I remember urging Rosie, who lived in Brighton, not to bother visiting David in hospital too often, because we would need her more when he was back at home, convalescent and bored. My attitude was: David has to go through a hellish six weeks but then he'll be fine.

And in fact his first week in the bone-marrow unit wasn't hellish at all – it was quite good fun. He had a minor operation on the first day to insert a Hickman line in his chest, and thereafter he had to spend a few hours every day on a drip, but in between he was free to come and go. Good foodie that he was, his first excursion was to Sainsbury's to lay in proper provisions – smoked salmon, prosciutto, figs. He asked me to bring his sketchbooks and painting things and to drive him to the secret garden in Regent's Park where he loved to paint. For several days, his only problem seemed to be boredom, so I organised a rota of friends to come and entertain him, and one night we even went out to a party. Again, when David told friends that he was in the middle of having a bone-marrow transplant, they simply didn't believe him – Geoffrey Wheatcroft said, well, *he* was in the middle of having root canal treatment which was far, far worse. The whole mood those first few days was one of almost gaiety. The only thing that brought us down to earth was when

David had to sign a consent form that said he understood there was only a 50 per cent chance of recovery. *Fifty* per cent! All we'd been told before was that there was a 10 per cent risk of his dying, from which we'd assumed that there was a 90 per cent chance of recovery. What happened in this other 40 per cent that wasn't dying and wasn't recovery? David, typically, signed the form without asking.

By the Friday, I noticed, David was beginning to sound a bit high, talking loudly about 'airhead nurses' and laughing too much. On the Saturday, he rang me very early, breathless with fear, saying he had not been able to pee in the night. I dashed over to UCH and found him almost gibbering with panic, unreachable, until the doctor came. The doctor explained that he was taking in so much liquid through his various drips, it naturally caused prostate problems but they would finish after the transplant. On Monday, he had a slight temperature and was told he must not go outdoors any more; on Tuesday, he complained of diarrhoea and aches and pains. He was in a strange, impatient, grandiose mood, often 'too busy' to talk to me. Instead, he gave me his hospital diary to read which was a wonderful account of a Proustian social whirl occasionally interrupted by this huffy wife who bustled in from time to time to spoil his fun.

On Thursday, 17 July, they started the transplant. Charles came to the 'blood room' to have his bone marrow 'harvested' and had to sit with his arm perfectly still for *four hours*, which can't have been much fun. But Charles was very good-humoured about it, and then our friend Eric Christiansen turned up and he and David and

Charles sat and talked about history while the nurses transferred Charles's blood to David. 'Don't you want to stay and watch?' they asked, but I couldn't wait to get out of there. Instead, I dashed to the Fresh Art Fair and bought a painting. It was the first time I had ever bought a painting without consulting David, and I felt oddly guilty, so much so that I didn't tell him. *He* was the art expert – it was as if I had taken a first, premature, step into independence.

The next day David looked absurdly well, with pink cheeks like Charles's, and we joked that perhaps he would turn into Charles and start wearing Boden clothes and talking about his 'chums'. But he was getting weaker all the time and that weekend he was declared neutropenic, meaning he had no immunity from infection. There was a big sign on his door saying visitors had to wash their hands and don a plastic apron – his brother Luke looked hilarious in his motorbike leathers with this titchy yellow apron stuck on the front. David by now was finding it hard to eat – he had no appetite and his mouth was sore with ulcers. He surprised me, though, by saying that he was never bored – I think because he was beginning to withdraw into a private, drugged, world.

By the end of the third week, Sunday, 27 July, David's mouth was so sore they were giving him morphine and he was eating only smoothies. His hair had started falling out and there were clumps of it all over his pillow; his hands and ankles were puffy; he was quaking with fever and barely coherent. Rosie, who hadn't seen him for a week,

155

was horrified by the change in him. On Monday, 28 July, David rang to say he was being transferred to the Middlesex kidney unit and I had better come over and pack his stuff. What! Why? Nobody had even mentioned his kidneys before but apparently they had stopped working and he had to have dialysis. The doctor admitted that kidney failure was rare and they didn't know why it had happened – it was the first time I had seen one of the transplant doctors looking rattled. David was whisked off in an ambulance while I stayed behind to pack. I thought I was meant to pack just an overnight bag but the nurses said no, I had to take everything, to vacate the room. It sounded as though they were washing their hands of him.

By the time I got over to the Middlesex and found the renal unit, David was already installed in a rather bleak room which I was appalled to see had no neutropenic sign on the door and nurses and porters seemed to be wandering in and out without washing their hands. I thought maybe I should stay the night, but David said very strongly I should leave – he seemed hostile and irritated by everything I did. So I went home and rang Charles and Luke and the daughters to tell them what had happened. I went to bed thinking, 'I could wake up a widow.'

But no – David was still alive in the morning but looking ghastly, with a bleeding mouth and puffy eyelids and no hair at all at the back. He was highly agitated and said a Chinaman had come in the night and stolen his Hickman line, and I thought, Oh God, he's barking. But later, when the consultant came round (with a Chinese doctor) he explained that they'd found his Hickman line was infected – hence his septicaemia – and removed it in the night. And there was a nice black nurse, Steve, who seemed able to calm David down – I certainly couldn't. He hooked David up to a dialysis machine which chugged away and sent David to sleep.

That first week in the renal unit, David was demented much of the time, sometimes paranoid, sometimes peremptory, often telling me off for being stupid. He had a theory of déjà vu he kept trying to explain – 'This is now and the loop only finishes when I'm dead' – and would get furious when I failed to understand and start again – '*This is now*' – until I wanted to scream. Later, I found pages of the same stuff in his diary. One night, apparently, he told Steve the nurse he had a son who had HIV – where did *that* come from? He also boasted to Steve and other nurses that I was a famous writer. Sometimes he thanked me effusively for being so 'caring'; other times he lambasted me for being so thick. I was grateful that Theo accompanied me on most of these visits and managed to 'humour' David when I couldn't – but then she would often break down in tears when we left the room. In one of his few moments of clarity, he said that he didn't think the bone marrow had taken. I said it was too early to know – they told us it would take two weeks – but privately I began to share his pessimism. Everything was going wrong.

By this time, I was having terrible dreams, barely sleeping at night but then crashing out at odd times during the day. Everything seemed out of joint. The papers were full of the terrible story of Dr Kelly, the MoD scientist who committed suicide. And it was so hot, day after day, the temperature rising relentlessly through the 80s into the 90s, it never seemed to cool even at night. Moreover it was a strange, muggy, misty heat, more like India before the monsoon than an English July. Another evil portent was that a huge dog fox had taken up residence in our garden and kept strolling along the walls as if patrolling the ramparts, which meant the cats would come crashing through the cat flap and pee in the house. We'd often had foxes in the garden before, but never one so big or so bold: I thought of him as Death and feared that one day he would come through the cat flap and take over the house.

Whenever I visited David at the Middlesex – and I was dutiful, I went at least once and often twice a day – I would start plotting to leave almost as soon as I arrived. I had my excuses – the meters that needed feeding, the phone calls that had to be made, the garden that needed watering (oh God, to think I put the garden first) – and was shamed one day when Steve, his lovely nurse, said that he could arrange a parking space for me. There were special 'compassionate' free parking spaces, he explained, and he would get me a chit for one because he knew it was so expensive parking in central London. I blushed and blushed because of course I could afford any amount of parking spaces. I just hated being in the hospital, hated being 'the patient's wife', hated the fact that I didn't know what to talk to David about – that when he tried to talk seriously, about dying for instance, I brushed him off, and that when I tried to tell him about everyday things, or friends who had called, I sounded like the silliest sort of airhead. He would ask politely about my work – what work? I was doing almost nothing. And I would ask about the nurses, and what had happened in the night, and how were his bowels. I was very aware that I was behaving wrongly, dashing in and out. Proper hospital wives sat like pylons at their husband's bedside, only occasionally moving to get a cup of tea. They stayed there all day, maybe even all night. David told me – I think because he sensed my guilt – that it was because they were from out of town and had nowhere to go in London, but I also felt it was because they were proper wives, the sort who stayed at their husband's side all their lives. Going down in the lift one day, one of them said to me, 'All we can do is give them our love', and I bared my teeth in a snarl. I just couldn't do this 'caring' lark – it made me feel inadequate and cross. I felt cross with David too, for deserting me.

But gradually, towards the end of the week, David seemed to come back. He was still very irritable, very querulous, by now institutionalised I suppose, but not, thank God, talking about his theories of déjà vu. Steve shaved his head so that there were no more depressing clumps on the pillow, and in fact he looked good with a skinhead. He started trying to read the papers again and do easy crosswords – oddly, though, he refused to let me bring his Walkman, and said he'd entirely lost his taste for classical music. At first he didn't even want any books but then I brought *The Poet's Tongue* and he started reading poetry again. One day he said his brain had gone, he couldn't remember all the poems he used to know by heart, he couldn't even remember 'The Rime of the Ancient Mariner'. I said, 'Oh, I'm sure you can – "It is an ancient Mariner,/ And he stoppeth one of three"' – and David went on from there, steaming effortlessly through however many million verses. When the children were small David was always reciting poetry on car journeys – he could keep going all the way from London to Cornwall – but when the children were older they would howl, 'Oh, not "The Rime of the Ancient Mariner"!' So he gradually stopped doing it and it was strange to hear him again after all these years. One of the nurses came in and was so amazed she went to fetch another nurse – they seemed to think reciting poetry was some supernatural gift like speaking in tongues.

On Sunday, 3 August, we were told that David had produced a few white blood cells – the transplant had taken! I rang Charles and Luke to tell them to crack open the champagne – he was on the way to recovery. There was still the small problem of his kidneys – he was having dialysis every other day – but the doctors seemed confident that his own kidneys would 'kick in' spontaneously in a week or two and then he could go home. Home! He had now been in hospital a month but it seemed more like a year.

When he stopped being demented, he became sentimental, often tearful. He talked about Richard's death and how much he missed him. I knew he was thinking about his own death, and wanting to talk about it. But for some reason I always blocked him, and became very brisk. One day a Cypriot haematologist came to see him (many of the top haematologists are Cypriots because Cyprus has an endemic blood disease, thalassaemia), and David asked where she was from and she said Famagusta and he started reminiscing about his happy childhood holidays on the beach at Famagusta, with tears in his eyes. And again I froze, as always annoyed by talk of that idyll, his childhood, which I always resented. I hated the idea that the beach at Famagusta still represented – more than half a century later – the happiest days of his life. I wanted to wail, 'But you *were* happy, I *know* you were happy, at least twice more than that, when Rosie and Theo were born.' Another time, he tried to tell me – again with tears in his eyes – that he was very grateful and touched by my 'loyalty' and I winced that he used the word loyalty rather than love. But maybe loyalty was the best I could do. I remember my father once angrily saying that I only came to visit him and my mother out of a sense of duty, and I snapped, 'Well, what else do you want?' and he said 'Love.' So simple really. But it was my father ('Fine words butter no parsnips') who had taught me to equate duty with love.

From then on, David got visibly better and stronger every day. I took him for little walks, first just to the end of the ward, but then down to the hospital garden – I had to buy him a sunhat because it was still boiling hot. The papers were saying the temperature would soon be over 100; right across Europe, people were dying from the heat. I bought a rocker sprinkler for the garden and my big treat, every evening, was sitting outside with a glass of wine, listening to the swish, swish of water pattering on leaves. The dog fox had gone.

David was declared no longer neutropenic so it was safe to have visitors and I became his social secretary again, arranging a busy rota of friends to keep him company. He said he wanted to get dressed and go outside, in the street, and the doctors said fine, so I brought his clothes from home. He was upset to find his feet were too swollen to fit into his shoes, and I had to buy him some horrible Velcro hiking sandals. On Friday, 8 August, he announced that we would go for a proper walk to see the Butterfield church, All Saints Margaret Street, that he loved. So we tottered along – him in his floppy sunhat and hideous sandals, me moaning as usual at having to walk so far, and to a church of all places. Of course I found All Saints repulsive – High Victorian, smells and bells – but David had expected that and teased me for my disdain. Then we went for coffee in an Italian café in Charlotte Street. I was nervous the whole time but he was confident and talking eagerly about his plans for the future – he wanted to paint bigger abstracts, have an exhibition. We saw the consultant when we got back, and asked what to expect – he said probably another week or two in the renal unit and then maybe a few days back in UCH, but David would certainly be out by the end of the month. I began to feel slightly panicky at the thought of having to nurse him at home but David said don't worry, if he needed proper nursing we'd hire someone – he knew I'd never make a Florence Nightingale. He was so happy and confident, it was as if he was now in a position to comfort me, to laugh at my failings.

On Saturday, 9 August, we'd arranged that Rosie would visit him in the morning, then our good friend Lesley Hoskins would take him lunch. Theo would drop by in the afternoon and I would visit him in the evening, when he had finished dialysis. So for me it was a whole free day and I went swimming at Highgate Ponds and planted Nicotiana plants and generally felt more relaxed than I had for weeks. In the evening I sat in the garden with the sprinklers on – it was the hottest day of the year – waiting for David to phone to say his dialysis was over. When the phone rang about seven I expected to hear David's voice. Instead I heard the ward sister saying that David was 'not responding'.

I drove to the hospital in half my usual time, scything through traffic, and found a team of medics jammed into David's room. He was lying on his side, twitching, his hands oddly clenched. He made no response when I held his hand and called his name. The medics said they thought he'd had a haematoma – a bleed to the brain – and was paralysed down his left side. They said the scanners at UCH were out of action because of the heat and they would take him to Queen Square Hospital for a scan. They said they would have to put him on a ventilator to move him. Meanwhile I rang Theo, who by chance was meeting friends nearby, and she came clicketing up to the ward in her kitten heels and lovely party frock and burst into tears when she saw David.

We said we would drive to Queen Square, rather than go in the ambulance, and went out into the pea-soup night, getting lost. Arriving at this vast, completely deserted hospital, with no sign of life apart from two security guards, we wondered if we'd come to the wrong place. But no, the guards said they were expecting an ambulance, but it would come to the back of the building not the front, so one of them led us through miles of empty corridors – the lights were on, computers whirring, but no people anywhere – and we waited in what seemed to be a children's playground (we found out afterwards it was the back of Great Ormond Street hospital) for the ambulance to arrive. At last it came – and we saw David bound to a stretcher, completely motionless, with a huge elephant tube over his face.

Theo and I followed the stretcher through the miles of corridors back to the front entrance, where a tetchy Australian woman said she was the 'patient co-ordinator' and she'd been looking for 'you guys' everywhere – it was exactly as if she was telling us off for being late at check-in. She took us down to a horrible tiny waiting room with freezing air conditioning and left us in the Arctic cold, while David was taken for his scan. After about an hour a kind Greek neurosurgeon came to explain that the scan showed extensive bleeding in the brain and that, while normally he would attempt to operate, it was obvious that any surgery would kill him. In retrospect I realise I was meant to say, 'Well if there's nothing you can do, let him go', but I was too confused, I didn't take the hint and said something like, 'Well, do what you can.' He said he would talk to David's other consultants from the bone-marrow and kidney departments who were on their way. Theo and I were so cold in the waiting room we went back up to the sweltering entrance hall and watched this procession of consultants arriving in their smart cars – a Porsche, an Aston Martin, a Mercedes – greeting each other with handshakes and slaps on the back. They disappeared down to the operating theatre and I kept walking past and peeping through the window till one of them saw me and drew down the blind. After another hour the neuro-surgeon came and said they had decided there was no point in operating and they would return David to the Middlesex intensive care. At this point the Australian trolley dolly perkily told me that 'You guys should go home and have a nice cup of tea and then tomorrow you can have a nice visit with the loved one.' I still regret that I was too exhausted to slap her.

Officially David's death occurred at noon on Sunday, 10 August, though even death, I learned, is not so clear cut. Theo and I grabbed a few hours sleep – poor Rosie, in Brighton, was waiting for the first train to London. We agreed to meet in intensive care as soon as Rosie could get there. Meanwhile I rang Charles very early, asking him to break the news to Maurice and try to contact Luke, who was somewhere in Scotland. Theo and I went to see David in intensive care and both promptly turned away. He was quite obviously dead, but hooked up to this horrible machine that made his chest rise and fall like some creaky Victorian waxwork. A doctor explained that he was effectively brain-dead, but they could keep him alive by machine for a day if other members of the family wanted to 'say their goodbyes'. I relayed all this to Charles, who relayed it to Maurice and eventually Luke, who raced back from Scotland to be with Maurice.

Theo and I had to go to the kidney unit to collect David's things – they were all piled in bags in a cupboard, another patient was already in his room, and there was no sign of Steve or the other nice nurses. The top kidney man came and explained what happened – the blood has to be thinned for dialysis so there was always a slight risk of bleeding to the brain. Back in intensive care, and now joined by Rosie, a team of doctors assembled to talk in euphemisms – basically it was just a case of deciding when to switch off the machine that was keeping David artificially alive. 'Switch off now,' we chorused. But, said the doctors, how did we feel about organ donation? Fine, we said, and they told us that an 'organ co-ordinator' would be in touch. But this meant, I realised later, that they had to keep David artificially alive in case any of his organs were needed. The organ co-ordinator rang in the afternoon with a weird questionnaire, asking among other things whether David had ever had sex with prostitutes, with animals, in Africa? 'Not all at once,' I joked – and heard her gasp of outrage at the other end. David would have laughed, but there was no David to hear. She told me, quite casually, that he had been declared dead at noon.

Postscript

When I was arranging David's funeral, the undertaker said that nowadays it was normal to have a photograph of 'the loved one' on the front of the Order of Service, and I said oh yes, good idea. I had hundreds of photos of David and, I thought, it would be easy to find a good one. But as I went through the family photo albums, I discovered with dismay that there were almost no photographs suitable for a funeral service, because most of them contained lobsters. Sometimes they were half lobsters surrounded by lettuce leaves on a plate, or sometimes they were live lobsters, just bought, kicking their legs at the camera, but either way the typical photograph consisted of a large lobster in the foreground with David pulling yum-yum faces in the background.

The reason lobsters featured so prominently in our family albums was because David loved eating them, and had taught the children to love them too, so we always had lobsters for our birthdays – Theo's on 5 March, Rosie's on 3 May, mine on 22 May, David's on 1 June – and I always took photos on these occasions. There was a similar succession of photos featuring David holding Christmas puddings with flaming brandy, but the lobster ones were definitely more appealing. In a way, I felt, a picture of David with a lobster would be ideal for his funeral card, a memory of countless happy family celebrations. And the vicar had told me at least three times that he wanted the funeral to reflect my wishes. I wished for a lobster! But no – David's father would be appalled, his brother Charles would be bewildered, even his younger brother Luke, keen lobsterphile though he was, might think it was a bit disrespectful. I must bow to convention in these matters and find a lobster-less picture.

I trawled on through the albums. There were plenty of pictures of David with the daughters on windy hilltops in the Lake District, or windy clifftops in Cornwall, but he was always wearing an anorak, with his hair blowing about. There were a few – very few – photographs of me and David together, usually dressed up for a party, both grinning cheesily and self-consciously at the camera. But they were invariably taken by the children and involved some camera-wobble. There were recent photographs of him painting in his studio but, because he was painting, he was turned away from the camera. In the end, I concluded that I possessed *no* straight portrait of David at all, and would have to forget the idea of a photograph on the funeral card.

But then when I opened one of the letters of condolence (how quickly one acquires the ghastly terminology! Of course I mean letters from friends) a photograph fell out and it was a lovely picture of David smiling with a backdrop of foliage behind. The letter was from Eric Christiansen and said it was taken at Eric's 60th birthday party, by his wife Sukey. Anyway, it was a perfect portrait and the printers said they could take out the foliage and put just David's face on the funeral card. So that's what they did, and it looked fine – though still, as I stared dry-eyed at the card throughout the funeral service, I regretted the missing lobster.

Afterwards several friends asked if I had copies of the photograph that they could keep, so I got a dozen printed. I kept the original – with foliage – and put it in a silver frame. I knew I ought to have a photograph of David on the mantelpiece, so I had that one, and a windy anorak one of him with the daughters in Cornwall. And then, as a compromise, I also had a lobster one, not framed, stuck pseudo-casually in the corner of the overmantel mirror. I felt I was doing all the correct widow things.

Some weeks later David's ex-colleague Paddy Scannell sent me the University of Westminster newsletter with an obituary of David. This was an extended version of his *Guardian* obituary and far from thrilling. But what was sensational was the photograph they used. It was one I had never seen before and showed David beaming, happy, exuberant and, I could tell, a bit drunk. He was smiling with deep fondness into the camera, or, more accurately, at the person holding the camera. I wrote to Paddy thanking him for the obituary and asking, as casually as I could, where the photograph came from and whether there was any chance of my getting a print? I explained that most of my photographs of David entailed lobsters and that straight portraits of him were rare. I asked – again, I hoped, casually – who took the photograph and on what occasion.

Paddy wrote back that the photograph belonged to an ex-colleague who was currently in the States but that he would get a copy for me as soon as she came back. She! Of course it was confirmation of what I suspected. Because it seemed obvious to me when I first saw the photo that David was in love with whoever took it. It was not just the affection in his smile – it was more the *confidence* that seemed to say, 'Okay, so I'm drunk, but I know you won't mind.' I had never asked David if he had affairs but I could chart, over the years, certain periods when he seemed to stay late at work, or when he had mysterious extra lectures or conferences to attend at the weekends. And when he was extra nice to me. Of course he was always nice to me, but there was sometimes an extra niceness that I thought betokened guilt.

Anyway I was now sure that I had proof of his infidelity – I could see that it would not exactly stand up in court but it was clear-cut proof to me. And the feeling it aroused in me was . . . Actually all sorts of confused feelings, but predominantly relief. Relief from a great weight of guilt that had been sitting on me like a boulder since David died. Guilt that I hadn't spent enough time with him in hospital, guilt that I was in the garden at home when he had his haematoma; guilt that I hadn't listened to his worries sympathetically, that I had been so brisk – *of course* you won't die, I'd told him, the doctors know what they are doing. And guilt, before that, aeons and aeons of guilt stretching back over all the years of our marriage. I was never a good wife; he should never have married me; he deserved someone nicer. But if he was unfaithful, ah, that made everything so much easier.

Losing my guilt was just what I needed at the time. It enabled me to stop obsessing about what happened in hospital and start thinking about how I could get on with my life. I'd been almost paralysed since David's death, but now I felt this great surge of energy in the course of which I organised an exhibition of David's work, had the house redecorated, built a fence, replanted the front garden. Some months later another letter from Paddy arrived, containing a photo. It took me a minute to recognise it – there was David beaming at the camera, slightly drunk, but there was another man next to him, also beaming at the camera, also slightly drunk, leaning on David's shoulder. Paddy's letter explained that the printers had managed to delete the other man when they used the photo for David's obituary. His name was Frank H, he was an ex-colleague of David's and the photograph was taken at his leaving party by his wife.

Good God. Frank H's leaving party had actually engraved itself on my memory as one of the nights years ago when David mysteriously stayed out late, and I remember thinking at the time, 'I have never even heard him mention a colleague called Frank H, so why does he need to attend his leaving party?' In fact if you had asked me to list all the reasons why I ever suspected David of being unfaithful, Frank H's leaving party – this mysterious colleague I'd never heard of till he left – would probably have come top of the list. And now here was Frank H – a pleasant enough bloke by the look of him – with his hand affectionately on David's shoulder, beaming at the camera just like David. And when I studied it carefully, I could see what the photograph showed. David was somewhat drunk but Frank H was *very* drunk – he was leaning

171

on David's shoulder probably to stop himself swaying. And David was smiling at Mrs H to reassure her, laughing about good old Frank, this dear old colleague who had got a bit squiffy. Thus, anyway, my reading of the picture, and why it now has pride of place on my mantelpiece. But, as I said before, I am a deep believer in the unknowability of other people – such was the lesson I learned from Simon all those years ago.

Thanks

I should like to thank Tony Lacey and all at Penguin for having faith in me; likewise, my agent Gill Coleridge. Thanks too to Ian Jack for publishing my original story in *Granta*, and to Nick Hornby, Amanda Posey and Finola Dwyer for making it into such a brilliant film. I am grateful to all my *Observer* colleagues, but especially John Mulholland, Jane Ferguson and Nicola Jeal, for turning a blind eye to my slacking while I finished this book. Friends who helped with encouragement are too many to list but they know who they are. And, as always, love and thanks to my daughters, Rosie and Theo, for their constant support.